Alaska's Father Goose

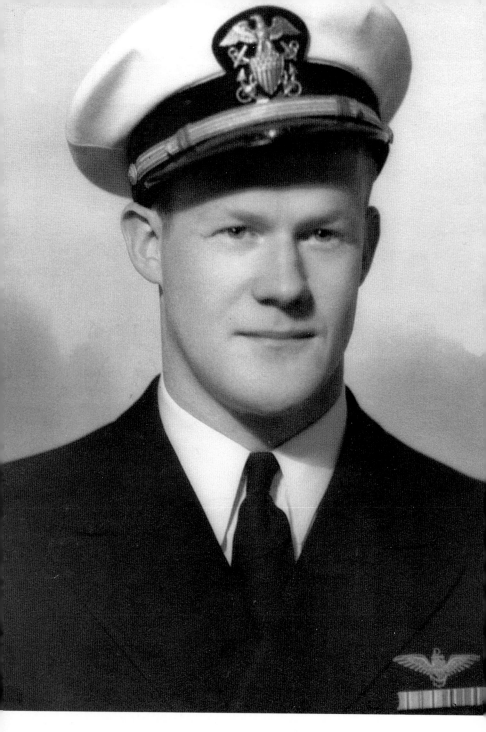

Lieutenant (JG) Bud Bodding

Alaska's Father Goose

Captain Gerald A. "Bud" Bodding:
A Career in Aviation

By Captain Gerald A. "Bud" Bodding
Edited by William F. Cass, Jr.

hancock
house

ISBN: 978-0-88839-651-8
Copyright © 2010 Eric Bodding

Cataloging in Publication Data

Bodding, Gerald A. (Gerald Alfred), 1917–2006.
  Alaska's Father Goose : Captain Gerald A. "Bud" Bodding :
  a career in aviation / by Gerald A. "Bud" Bodding ;
  edited by William F. Cass, Jr.

  Includes index.
  Issued also in electronic format.
  ISBN 978-0-88839-651-8

  1. Bodding, Gerald A. (Gerald Alfred), 1917–2006.
2. Bush pilots—Alaska—Biography. 3. United States.
Navy—Airmen—Biography. 4. Aeronautics, Commercial—
Alaska—History. I. Cass, William F., 1942– II. Title.

TL540.B62A3 2009   629.13092   C2009-904713-6

Editor: Theresa Laviolette
Production: Mia Hancock
Cover Design: Mia Hancock

Published simultaneously in Canada and the United States by

HANCOCK HOUSE PUBLISHERS LTD.
19313 Zero Avenue, Surrey, B.C. Canada V3S 9R9
(604) 538-1114 Fax (604) 538-2262

HANCOCK HOUSE PUBLISHERS
1431 Harrison Avenue, Blaine, WA U.S.A. 98230-5005
(604) 538-1114 Fax (604) 538-2262

www.hancockhouse.com
sales@hancockhouse.com

Contents

Preface

This is the remarkable real-life story of Gerald A. "Bud" Bodding of Ketchikan, Alaska, in his own words. Top-ranked by his peers and passengers alike as one of the true "greats" of the rugged Last Frontier's bush pilot flying lore, Bud fittingly presents his personal saga in typical Captain Bodding matter-of-fact style. He leaves it to the reader's imagination to ponder on the emotive aspects of his hard-earned, thirty-five-year Alaska flying career as we ride along on a wondrous flying tour back through the mists of time to a different era. Bud warmly accords us the much-vied-for copilot's seat for an exciting in-the-cockpit view of his civilian and Navy flying experiences around Southeast Alaska's Panhandle and the long Aleutian Chain, two of the world's absolutely most unforgiving aviation environments. This long-awaited pilot's autobiography is also a great book about a special breed of people who take great pride in calling themselves Alaskans: fellow sportsmen, adventurers, and entrepreneurs. Bud was all of those. His industrious "can do" generation employed a pioneer-spirit work ethic to tame Alaska's wilderness and to successfully defend it in time of war. One was only as good as one's word, and the big deal-making handshake was standard business protocol back then. Bud and his peers embraced traditional family values, strong bonds of friendship, and fairness to define their unique lifestyle, while "playing hard" in their outdoor paradise to rejuvenate.

Bud Bodding was a genuine lifetime Alaskan, born and raised in the capital city of Juneau. His scope of involvement in Alaskan aviation was comprehensively deep and mostly exclusive to the region. He witnessed the very origins of Alaska's now legendary bush-pilot history by watching pioneer Roy F. Jones and his Curtiss flying boat, *Northbird,* in operation, and got his initial plane ride in Juneau's first airplane — a JN4D, later modified and flown there as Alaska's only seaplane "Jenny." Going from roustabout to mechanic in short order, Bud joined ranks with the pioneers of Alaska's seaplane country and realized his destiny as a pilot, soloing during early training with Juneau's first flying club. From then on, after earning his commercial license down south at the then fabled Ryan School of Aeronautics in San Diego, everything was "up" for Bud's ambition.

He became an Alaskan bush pilot with great success through his skill and careful by-the-book philosophy, along with military training and wartime experiences. Happily, Lady Luck was Bud's ally throughout those inevitable close calls associated with any lengthy flying career and during some truly incredible twists of fate. He logged just under 24,000 hours total flying time in twenty different types of aircraft while flying all sorts of passengers: from admirals and movie stars to everyday people and their goods during routine and emergency flights.

Bud Bodding's all-time favorite aircraft was the sturdy, twin-engine Grumman Goose amphibian, which he first flew early in the Second World War. The Goose became the dominant seaplane workhorse for Southeast Alaska for almost thirty years after the war, and was the backbone of the large competitor fleets of Ellis Air Lines of Ketchikan and Alaska Coastal Airlines of Juneau. The legendary amphibian also flew with Coastal–Ellis and Alaska Airlines; twenty of those hardy birds saw service during their years in those airlines' revenue service. Bud's lifelong love affair with the Goose was true and complete (so much so, that, unlike most of his contemporaries, he opted not to check out in either the upgraded turbopropjet modified "Super-Goose" or to re-qualify in the big twenty-four-passenger PBY Catalina that he had flown during the war). Nor did he choose to move up to fly the big jets after Alaska Airlines took over the company in 1968. His heart belonged to the Goose.

The twin-piston-engined Goose became Bud's trademark, earning him the immortal title of "Father Goose." Bud logged over 18,000-hours flying the Grummans, before retiring on October 28, 1972, following a final scheduled run to Prince of Wales Island stops in Alaska Airlines' Goose N4772C. Bud was a survivor — the epitome of the old cliché, Old Bold Pilot, (although he likely did not consider himself being audacious by any stretch). Recognizing the advent of regional jet airliner travel in Southeast

Alaska with new airports in Sitka, Wrangell, and Petersburg, and chafing under the weight of new large corporate management styles and conglomerated, diluted seniority, Bud figured it was time to call it quits and never piloted a plane again.

He subsequently devoted himself to his family and running a charter fishing boat business. He is remembered by those who worked under him as always being a fair and consistent boss, while expecting his staff to put forth their best efforts towards earning their paycheck. New-hire pilots recall Bud, at that time company chief pilot and Vice President Operations–Southeast, making it standard operating procedure to greet them upon first arrival in Ketchikan and then immediately helping them and their families get promptly settled into the community.

My initial contact with Father Goose was via letter in early March 1981 when I first got interested in researching Southeast Alaska aviation history for writing and illustration projects as a freelancer followed by writing many of the old timers for their first-hand accounts. I had already learned that it was essential do one's best to get the facts right when dealing with matters of history. Relying solely upon old newspaper clippings, magazine articles, or even published books for information was potentially troublesome. Most people appreciate accuracy when telling their stories in word or picture, including Bud Bodding. He was always kind and eager to help me, or anyone else who was sincerely interested in learning about the local history. Bud freely shared his input, opinions, and scrapbook archives, and was always supportive of my endeavors over the years of promoting Alaskan aviation history. I appreciated his keen recall of factual events, which helped me successfully navigate through primary research's many shoal waters.

Back in 1985, when former Ellis Air Lines (EAL) company employees held a big reunion gathering in Ketchikan, I teamed up with my friend and fellow airline historian, the late Walt Goodwin, Sr., to put on a special exhibit at the local Tongass Historical Society Museum, culminating in a historical slide show program at the VFW Hall banquet finale. Walt, a Coastal–Ellis vet, dispatched for Alaska Airlines in Ketchikan. He had wisely saved many discarded company history files during the Alaska Southeast Airlines post-merger housecleaning, becoming a "keeper of the flame" in the process. Walt was eager to introduce me to all the great old hands from the Goose-flying era, but regrettably had to cancel at the last minute. "Father Goose" came forward and graciously accorded my wife Linda and me a nice warm welcome and took us under wing to meet the celebrative crowd. That wonderful encounter sparked a long and valued friendship with the Bud and Betty Bodding family.

After rubbing elbows with so many great aviation old timers at the EAL reunion, I came away more inspired than ever by their personal stories about the golden era of the Grumman Goose in Southeast Alaska's aviation history, and wondered why nobody had thought to save one for posterity to proudly display in a local museum.

This obvious oversight prompted my conceiving the "Save The Goose!" Project, launched in November 1988 to generate community interest in support of finding and acquiring an authentic, regional fleet veteran Grumman Goose for permanent indoor museum exhibit in Ketchikan. The Grumman Goose was an ideal choice for a dynamic museum centerpiece because it would perfectly represent the unique Southeast Panhandle island lifestyle and honor aviation's importance in Alaska's development.

The immortal amphibian was a perfect aviation icon to represent all the great aircraft types and air services in Southeast's history and the people who sacrificed so much to establish the Alaska bush flying tradition. Ketchikan was certainly blessed by providence in late 1992, when our successful fundraising marathon returned home the original Ellis Air Lines Grumman: N88821 — the company's "Mother Goose" — from nearby Prince Rupert, British Columbia. It did not matter that she came back a cannibalized old wreck, needing a lengthy total rebuild on top of restoration. On November 8, 1992, "Ole 821" was met by a smiling entourage of her original airline family, led by Bob Ellis and Bud Bodding, which kicked off a wild, one-day-only winter air show celebration. Three Gooses were flown-in for the event, including Shell Simmons' original Alaska Coastal Airlines Goose: N48550, operated by Portland businessman, Larry Teufel, and previously flown by Bud during the Coastal–Ellis and Alaska Airlines eras. On that remarkable day, twenty years after retirement, Captain Bud Bodding returned to the cockpit to fly once again. As Larry's copilot in 550, Bud served as the air show Grand Marshal, to everyone's delight (including his own!).

The Tongass Historical Society's Goose was Bud's pet project in his later years and is, indeed, a remarkably fitting memorial to him and his fellow Alaskan aviation pioneers. Blue skies forever, Father Goose!

Don "Bucky" Dawson
Save-the-Goose! Project Coordinator
Tongass Historical Society

The Grumman Goose

Grumman, of Bethpage, Long Island, New York, will probably always be best known for its long series of Navy aircraft, especially fighters. The company was also well known for its involvement with amphibious aircraft, dating from 1933 when it introduced the single-engine JF Duck. Grumman's first twin-engine amphibian was the little Widgeon. Powered by two Ranger engines of 200 horsepower each, the Widgeon was developed for both the civil and military market. The Goose was introduced strictly for the upscale sportsman and commuter segments of the civil market as the Grumman Model G21 in 1937, but was soon serving with the Navy and Coast Guard as well as the Royal Air Force and Royal Canadian Air Force.

The Goose was powered by two Pratt and Whitney radial engines of 450 horsepower, the same engines that powered the Army Air Force and Navy basic trainer in World War Two, the

Turbo Goose conversion.

Vultee BT-13 Valiant, and the classic DeHavilland Beaver seaplane. The Goose could be configured to seat a maximum of eleven passengers and pilot.

The Goose wingspan was nearly fifty-one feet and gross weight came to roughly 12,500 pounds. After the war, many Goose aircraft were retrofitted with stronger engines. The latest conversion is the turbo-prop equipped Turbo-Goose. Approximately 345 Goose aircraft were produced, but only a handful remains in service today.

After World War Two, Grumman also built larger, more powerful amphibians, notably the Mallard and Albatross, but it is the Goose that Alaskans remember best.

Acknowledgements

We are most grateful, ultimately, to our father for his decision to pass his experiences on to his children, grandchildren, and great grandchildren in the form of a personal memoir before his death. With so many members of the "greatest generation" gone and the others disappearing so rapidly, we are indeed fortunate to have a personal account of those men and women who grew up in the Depression, fought in and worked at home to support the Second World War, and came home to build families and careers that have made America such a remarkable country.

Our thanks go to Eddy Haynes, master of that remarkable Internet website devoted to the Grumman Goose — Goose Central — for the essential and time-consuming task of transcribing Dad's handwritten rough draft into a word-processed file. Shortly after Dad died, we decided that the story had to reach an audience much wider than just the Bodding family and immediate friends.

Out of the blue several months later, William F. Cass, Jr. (son of Dad's closest flying school friend, Bill Cass) contacted us. He had read on the Internet about Dad's passing. Bill, who had met Dad in September 2003, generously offered his time as copy and photo editor, while also assuming responsibility for developing publisher proposals and, subsequently, liaison with Hancock House Publishers.

Early in the game, it became apparent that more pictures were needed to go along with the book. Although Dad had amassed quite a collection of photos relating to his flying experiences over the years, many were loaned out and never returned. Thus, it became a bit of a scramble to locate more pictures essential for the book. We are indebted to Leon Snodderly, Pete Ellis, Mike Ellis, Sue Bramstedt, Lois Hickey, Peggy MacInnis, Ted Spencer, and Marilyn Gropstis Chase for all of their help in tracking down and acquiring some of those rare photos.

We are also very grateful to Alaskan aviation historian Don

"Bucky" Dawson for writing the introduction. Dad would have enjoyed every word because it uniquely reflects his core existence: Juneau origins, flying in the Golden Age of Aviation, wartime naval aviation, pioneering commercial aviation, adventurer, sportsman, and family man. The Tongass Historical Society could not have picked a better man to head a project (Save the Goose!) so central to the latter years of Father Goose himself.

Finally, special appreciation goes to David Hancock and his staff at Hancock House Publishers for adding *Alaska's Father Goose* to their distinguished list of Pacific Northwest wildlife, nature, adventure, aviation, and biography titles.

JIM BODDING
ERIC BODDING
SHEILA HAYES BODDING

PART ONE:
THE EARLY YEARS 1917–1942

I: Growing Up In Juneau

On August 24, 1917, at the home of Olaf and Anna Bodding, 822 B Street, Juneau, Alaska, twins Geraldine and Gerald Bodding were born fifteen minutes apart. Geraldine was the first arrival. Apparently to avoid confusion, I was nicknamed "Bud." To date, that is the name I answer to.

My first introduction to aircraft was in 1923 when my dad took me down to the city float to view the Roy Jones flying boat *Northbird*. I recall a couple of men pulling the prop through trying to start the engine. We watched for quite a period of time, but they had no success in getting the engine to start. I remember going home and making a crude model of the airplane.

In 1929 the Navy had a number of Loening amphibian aircraft stationed at Juneau along with the minesweeper, USS *Gannet*. For a while they utilized the government dock where the aircraft were hoisted out. This was not far from home, so I used to walk down and gaze at the planes. I recall one of the pilots, Lt. Burnett, who was my hero.

In the spring of 1929, when I was eleven, Dr. Vance Howe, a local osteopath, purchased an OX-5-powered Curtiss JN-4 "Jenny" aircraft that had been stored at a warehouse in Douglas, just across the Gastineau Channel from Juneau. My dad, who owned a transfer business, was hired to haul it from the Juneau Admiral Line dock, nine miles out the highway to a flat adjacent to Kendler's Dairy. Since it was a Saturday with no school, I got to go along. It took two trips, including the first one with the tailskid on a truck bed towing the aircraft fuselage backwards; the other trip handled

Juneau during Alaska's "Golden Age of Aviation," circa 1930s.

the wings. I stayed out with the fuselage while the trip for the wings was made, and by then I was hooked.

School was out in a few days, and I hitchhiked out to the field to watch the first flight of the Curtiss, now christened *Totem*. It was to be used for flight lessons with instructor pilot Lyle Woods. He impressed me as a very dapper sort of person with his high boots, or puttees. The first flight was of short duration — just to take off and circle around to land — but on approach, something did not work out. Pilot Woods came in low, clipped a barbed wire fence, and missed the approved landing area, which was marked by a large canvas tarp. The aircraft went up on its nose, breaking the propeller. Considering transport in those days, it took a couple of weeks to get a replacement.

In the meantime, my good friend Cliff Berg joined me, and we used to hitchhike out practically every day to see what was going on. Once, we camped out for a full week in a tent that had been erected on the landing field. Dr. Vance and pilot Woods liked us being there because we kept the cows away. The animals had a habit of poking their horns through the wings and tail surfaces.

Pilot Woods was quite a ladies' man. On one occasion he came to the field accompanied by a very pretty lady. By this time he figured he owed Cliff and me a ride in the airplane, so why not take care of the situation all at once? He put the lady in the front seat and me on her lap. With helmet, goggles, etc., we took off, made a short flight, and then flew back and landed. Cliff then had his turn. It was the same deal — on the lady's lap. I do not recall if the seat belt went around us both, but anyhow the air was smooth. Other than that first incident with the broken propeller, everything went well. However, for the rest of that summer nobody learned to fly.

Around the middle of September, the aircraft was dismantled and stored in a warehouse in Juneau. The aircraft was sold to Shell Simmons, Wally Bergstrand, and Fred Soberg, and by the next summer, the aircraft was assembled on property owned by Danner's Dairy. A friend of Shell's was pilot on the test hop. He had a bit more flying experience than Shell, but on landing he over-ran the field and ended up in a pile of stumps. The right wing was washed out. The remains of the aircraft were stored in a Juneau warehouse, and throughout the winter months the three partners rebuilt the plane. They installed a spare set of shorter wings, a single wooden float, and home-built wing floats. During all the changes, I hung around and did minor things to help out.

The job was finished in the summer of 1931 and the plane was re-assembled utilizing a seaplane float adjacent to the rock dump. The test hop was made in Juneau early on a nice summer day. I knew about it and got up early to watch. Fred Soberg went along with Shell Simmons. The plane got airborne, but the flight was of short duration, since it was quite tail heavy. The problem was corrected by moving the main float forward.

I hung around quite a bit that summer and still recall one incident when Simmons and Soberg returned after a flight. Soberg got out of the forward cockpit with the engine still running, jumped for the float, and was hit by the revolving propeller. He suffered a cut on his forehead and lost a thumb. Simmons took me for a ride in the Jenny before the summer was over.

The main float on the aircraft was made of laminated wood. After sitting out all summer in the rain, it became water-soaked and heavy. Simmons took a local photographer, Fred Ordway, and his heavy camera equipment on a photographic trip. After a long run, they finally got airborne but climbed very little. The aircraft, with full power on, finally settled back on the water. That ended the flying days for the converted Jenny. Neither Bergstrand nor Soberg ever soloed.

In the late twenties and early thirties, a number of attempts were made to start summer seaplane operations out of Juneau, including Gorst Air Transport, Alaska Southern Airways, Alaska Washington Airways, and Pacific Alaska Airways. I used to hang around all the various outfits in hopes of somehow getting a ride. I did luck out once, going on a test hop in a Gorst Air Transport flying boat with owner Vern Gorst as pilot.

In 1932, Shell Simmons started the Juneau Flying Club and

Skylark, an Aeromarine Klemm owned by the Gastineau Flying Club.
The Klemm, produced in the US under license from Daimler–Klemm in Germany, was originally built as a glider. The last model was powered by a 65-hp engine.

Flying the mail, Stinson SM2A.

Stinson SM2A, *Patco.*

ARCTIC OCEAN

RUSSIA

E

Bering Strait

ALASKA

Anchorage

Va

Bering Sea

Aleutian Islands

Gu

PACIFIC OCEAN

purchased an Aeromarine Klemm aircraft on floats. A hangar was built north of Juneau above the high tide mark. Launching the plane was quite a chore; there was a steep ramp out of the hangar with planks anchored to the low water mark. Again, I used to hang around and be as helpful as possible, and before the summer was over, Simmons took me for a ride and gave me my first flying lesson. Quite a number of Juneauites soloed in the Klemm in subsequent years, including my close friend Bill "Sonny" Lund.

In late summer 1935, the days of the Aeromarine Klemm ended when Dr. L.P. Dawes, a local surgeon and politician, "stubbed his toe" (landed nose too far down, jamming the front end of the pontoons into the water) on a landing at Berner's Bay. The aircraft was demolished.

In the meantime, Shell Simmons had taken a job with Panhandle Air Transport as a pilot. They had one airplane, a Stinson SM2A, the Patco. Shell was determined to be the first to establish year around air service in Juneau, but things were really tough the first winter. At one time he was at home in bed recovering from an appendix operation. It was a blustery "Taku" day and I remember him saying, "If I had a one-way fare to Funter Bay, I would go down and take it."

In 1935, I graduated from Juneau High School (not with honors); I was a lousy student, mainly due to a lack of interest. The school principal called in each graduating senior for a little talk. When my turn came I was asked what my plans were for the future. "I want to be an airplane pilot," was my reply, but he was not impressed.

That winter I was only working part-time as a truck driver for my dad. A friend of mine talked me into taking a trip with him to visit his hometown in eastern Washington. We caught the Northland Transportation steamer *North Sea* to Seattle. At Petersburg, a very pretty young lady, Betty Hofstad, boarded with her grandmother. They were en route to Bellingham, Washington, where Betty was to enter school. Betty and I spent time together talking, enjoying the scenery, and dancing in the evening.

Eastern Washington had no interest for me, and I soon caught

Bud at 18, driving for his father's trucking company.

Bud Bodding and Bill Lund with the Lockheed Vega.

a bus back to Seattle where I stayed at the Stevens Hotel for one dollar a night, and then caught the *North Sea* back to Juneau.

I went back to part-time truck driving for my dad and Sommers Construction Company. Sommers had a contract for road building at Seward for the summer of 1937, and I was scheduled to go there. My interest was in aviation though, and with summer approaching, Simmons offered me a job as "general roustabout," which also included riding along as what we called "flight mechanic" on numerous trips. My pay was ninety dollars per month. Eight-hour days were unheard of. On numerous occasions I would be down to launch the airplane at 5:00 a.m. and at 10:00 p.m. I would still be there cleaning the plane and pumping the floats.

Business prospered and a Bellanca Senior Pacemaker and a

Bud operating Alaska Air Transport's radio. May 1937.

Marine Airways' Bellanca Pacemaker. *KEITH PETRICH PHOTO.*

Lockheed Vega at Juneau.

Marine Airways Bellanca Pacemaker. *GORDON WILLIAMS PHOTO VIA JIM RUOTSALA.*

Hoisting the Lockheed Vega at Alaska Air Transport's Juneau hangar.

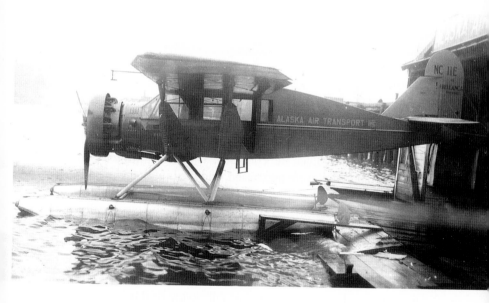

Alaska Air Transport's Bellanca Skyrocket.

The Gastineau Flying Club's two-place Aeronca C-3, *Oompah,*
was powered by a 40-hp engine.

Lockheed Vega were added to the "fleet." Pilots Jim Rinehart and
Frank Barr also joined the company. The Juneau Motor Company
building and dock were purchased, and the building was converted
to a hangar. A hoist to lift the aircraft was installed on the dock; the
unit consisted of a stiff leg and boom, cable, and electrically operated winch.

There were some problems with the set up, however. The
Bellanca was lifted to the dock, but the next morning when Shell
attempted to lower the aircraft to the water, the brake did not work and
the plane made pretty much a "free fall" to the float below. Both front
struts were broken and the propeller was bent. Afterwards, a number

Lloyd Jarman and Bill Lund launching the Aeronca C-3. 1936.

Air-to-air shot of Bud flying the Gastineau Flying Club's Aeronca.
August 15, 1938. *KEITH PETRICH PHOTO.*

of changes were made. A sophisticated brake system was installed, and also a very heavy concrete block with chains on all four corners, to hook on the lifting eyes on the aircraft, was incorporated. The purpose was to assist in lowering the cable when the aircraft was not attached.

On one occasion, an employee had lowered the Lockheed down to the water. I tied the plane to the float below and unhooked the chains. I seated myself in the aircraft and proceeded to warm up the engine. Imagine my surprise when, gazing up, I observed the concrete block descending, directly overhead. I immediately shut the engine down and made a quick exit through the rear pilot's door. The operator of the hoist had left the switch in the up position and walked away. The block went up against the pulley on the end of the boom and then blew the master fuse. The brake did not hold completely, allowing the concrete block to slowly descend until it rested on top of the Lockheed wing. Nothing was damaged, but I shudder to think what would have happened if the brake would have completely failed, or if the cable had broken.

I enjoyed my work at Alaska Air Transport. There was something new every day. On one occasion, a lady chartered the Bellanca for a trip to Seattle. Since there was lots of room, I got to go along. Just prior to landing at Lake Union, Seattle, the canoe paddle, which was standard equipment, broke loose from its bracket and damaged the water rudder pull-up cables.

The next day, Shell dropped me off to repair the cables while he did some shopping. I completed the job and about 5:00 p.m. Shell, accompanied by two nurse trainee acquaintances, picked me up. Shell and I had two adjoining rooms at the Vance Hotel. The plan was go to the hotel where I would clean up and change clothes, and then we would go to dinner.

I joined the group in Shell's room where I was introduced to a drink called a "nosedive." The drink consisted of a shot glass placed in a water glass. The shot glass was filled to the brim with whiskey. The water glass was then filled with ginger ale to the top of the whiskey glass. The idea was to "bottoms up," tasting only the ginger ale. With my empty stomach — and I do not know how many nosedives — I soon became dizzy and quite sick. Needless to say, I did not make dinner. We all learn by doing. Shell never let me forget it. For along time afterwards, at gatherings he would say, "Shall I tell them about Seattle?"

Another time, also in the Bellanca, I went along on a charter trip to Skagway to pick up a salesman and his bags. We never got there. En route, we ran into fog conditions, so we landed to await better weather. With a little improvement we took off, but right after becoming airborne, Shell hollered, "Something broke!" and cut the throttle. Down we came to a hard landing, almost stubbing the floats' noses. We proceeded to the beach where we found one of the upper elevator control cables had broken. As usual, Shell had the answer. He opened a panel to the tail section, fastened a rope to the broken elevator cable, and put me in the back seat to hold it. My instructions were to pull the line if it went slack, and to slack off if it got tight. We flew the airplane back to Juneau that way. For sometime afterward, I was referred to as the "human splice."

Returning to the spring days of 1936, a local Juneau group including Bill Lund, Mary Joyce, Tony Karnes, Mark Storms, Joe Storms, and me, formed the Gastineau Flying Club. Shell Simmons "spark plugged" the deal and offered Jim Rinehart of Alaska Air Transport as an instructor. As I recall, we put in $600 per person and purchased a new thirty-six-horsepower C-3 Aeronca. It was flown from the factory to Seattle where floats were installed prior to loading aboard a steamship for transport to Juneau. The total cost delivered was $2,800. That summer all club members soloed and were traditionally dunked, clothes and all, in the waters off the seaplane float. My total dual-time before solo was four hours and forty-two minutes. After that, I just flew solo and probably did not learn too much.

One of the flying club rules was that our flying range limit was the Gastineau Channel in the Juneau area. One nice summer day, Bill Lund, without saying anything to anyone, took off and ended up in Sitka. While on the water, Shell Simmons flew in and caught Bill. I happened to be down on the float when Lund returned to Juneau to be confronted by Simmons. Shell was quite upset and told Lund, "You will never fly for me or anyone else in Alaska." Shortly thereafter we held a meeting of the flying club and agreed cross-country flights would be allowed with restrictions.

Bill Lund went to Seattle and received his commercial pilot's

Bud Bodding flying the Aeronca C-3 over Lake Florence.
KEITH PETRICH PHOTO.

Bud Bodding, Bob Daly, and Ray Robinson with the
Lockheed Vega.

Bud and mechanic, Ray Robinson, with Alaska Air
Transport's Vega.

license. He started flying for Alaska Airlines in the early days. As
its top pilot, he was in command of Alaska Airlines' first commercial passenger flight to Siberia.

Winter seaplane flying in the Juneau area was sometimes a
problem, and Taku winds (high winds caused by the mountainous
terrain in Southeast Alaska) one of the main restrictions. I recall
one really windy, nasty day. Shell had a charter to pick up passengers at the Taku River Lodge area. After pacing the dock for a
while, he could stand it no longer. We were told to put the
Lockheed in the water. We put numerous ropes on the airplane and
enlisted the help of a number of passersby to help lower the aircraft. Shell and I got in and departed the float. My instructions
were to climb up on the wing. Taku winds hit from all sides. I was
to watch for gusts and scramble out onto the upwind wing with
nothing to hang on to and no life preserver.

We made it across the bay where the wind was less gusty. We
then took off for a very bumpy ride to the Taku River area. With
the gusty winds and ice flows, it was impossible to land. Back to
Juneau we flew and landed north of the Juneau–Douglas Bridge. I
went up onto the wing for a repeat of the taxi-out adventure. With

Bud on the Ryan flight line with an STA.

more recruited help, we got the plane back on the dock and into the hangar. My job was not done, because I had to clean the salt spray off the aircraft and pump the floats. Incidentally, with much better weather the next day, we completed the trip.

In December 1937, my dad decided to go into the oil delivery business. The town of Juneau was rapidly converting from coal-burning stoves and furnaces. I was advised that if I went to work for a period of one year for Bodding Transfer I could go to flying school, which sounded good to me. Accordingly, on the first day of January 1938 I started my new job. My first oil delivery was in answer to a 4:00 a.m. call on a cold, windy morning. A family was out of oil and feared that their pipes would freeze without heat. I promptly delivered the oil and was told that payment would be made the next day when our office was open. We never received payment, and the family moved out of town. I found out they were deadbeats and had burned at least two other oil companies. That was an important lesson.

During my stint as an oil truck driver I was also introduced to coal sacking and packing. There were nine sacks to a thousand pounds. My dad would take orders for packing coal up flights of steps that other transfer companies would turn down. That just made my back and legs stronger. As I recall, we were paid twenty-five cents a sack for delivery whether we dumped it in a bin along side the road or packed it up 100 flights of stairs.

While I was working with Bodding Transfer, I continued flying the Aeronca. Our office was adjacent to the hangar, and during slack periods I would go out and fly for a half hour or so; then, too, there were days off. With the Gastineau Channel restrictions removed I would sometimes make solo flights for overnight fishing trips to various lakes.

I still hung around with the local aviation group. One evening, Shell and I, together with another person who was a purser on an Alaska Steamship vessel docked in Juneau overnight, were sitting in the Triangle Bar, when Shell had a phone call advising him that there was a medical emergency at the Todd Cannery. It was a nice evening, but dark with no moon. The three of us went down to the hangar, prepared the Lockheed for flight, and away we went to Todd, where Shell made a good landing. We taxied in and tied to the

Second Lieutenant William F. Cass, December 1942.

float. There were a number of people standing around with flash-lights. Shell inquired, "Where is the patient?" Someone answered, "Here I am!" and walked up to the aircraft. He had a bandaged arm, but without any sign of blood. We took off without problem.

At Juneau, someone had alerted the townspeople, and when we arrived there were numerous cars lined up on the government dock with their lights shining over the bay. That was a nice gesture, but all it did was cause a glare on the water. Shell chose to land further down the bay.

At the float, the patient refused ambulance service, and went into the office and paid for his charter. The last we saw of him, he was walking up the street, possibly to the nearest bar. So much for that "emergency." That was probably the first intentional night trip for seaplanes into or out of Juneau.

II: Commercial Pilot

At the end of December 1938, I informed my dad that I was board-ing an Alaska Steamship boat on January 1 for Seattle and on to San Diego, California, to attend the Ryan School of Aeronautics. At Seattle, I went to the bus station, paid an eighteen-dollar fare, and took the long ride to San Diego.

I checked in at the Golden West Hotel, a rather sleazy but cheap hotel. I had heard that Lyle Woods, the Jenny pilot men-tioned above, resided in San Diego and worked for a dental supply company, so, being alone in a large city, I went to its office to look him up. I was told he had been killed a week before in an airplane accident. I think if I'd had the eighteen-dollar bus fare I would have returned to Seattle, since I really had that lonesome, homesick feeling. Instead, I took part of my few remaining dollars and wired home for some money care of Golden West Hotel.

The next day I went out to Lindbergh Field and contacted the

Bud and a Ryan Sport Cabin (SC) used for cross-country training. June 1939.

Bud logged ten hours in the Travel Air 6000 at Ryan.

Pan American pilots, Gene Myring and Joe Crosson, with Fairchild in Juneau.

Bud with one of the Ryan School of Aeronautics' STAs. Spring 1939.

The Ryan STA (Sport Trainer, Model A), still one of the most beautiful airplanes ever built.

First Lieutenant Wm. F. Cass with B-25 Mitchell medium bomber. Late 1943.

Glacier landing, Reeve Airways Fairchild 71.

Ryan School of Aeronautics. I was told my cost to complete the commercial course would be $1,900.42, which resulted in another wire home for money.

In the meantime, the school found me a spot in the Balboa Park area where room, breakfast, and dinner was twenty-eight dollars per month. There were two other Ryan students there, and one had a car. This worked out quite well, but there were times I had to walk home, so I soon found a place closer to the airport for the same room and board.

My best friend at the Ryan school was Bill Cass, a young man from Syracuse, New York, who also was taking the commercial course. In early June, his mother, sister, and an aunt came out to California, and I was invited to go along with them as their guest on a weekend trip to Los Angeles where we stayed at the Ambassador Hotel.

The ground school and flying at Ryan took well over six months, and was a very complete and concise course. In addition to my previous flight time, I was required to log 125 hours at the flight school. Flying was mostly done in the Ryan STA aircraft, which was a two-cockpit, low-wing aircraft powered with a Menasco engine. Other aircraft included a Ryan SC, a four-place,

Reeve's Fairchild on the beach at Valdez in January
1940, prior to installing skis.

enclosed cabin plane with a Warner radial engine, and a six-place
Travel Air aircraft.

My course included ten hours aerobatics in the STA, ten hours
instrument training "under the hood" in the STA, ten hours night
flying in the SC, and ten hours of landings and takeoffs in the big
old Travel Air, plus a number of cross-country flights in the STA
and SC.

Of interest, when flying around the field in the Travel Air, the
circuit was short. The old Wright engine was rather "dirty," throw-
ing quite a bit of oil on the windshield, which resulted in poor forward vision on a long trip. Our standard cleaning procedure was to
pull up on landing, reach out the sliding window, and wipe off the
windshield.

Bob Ellis earned his Navy commission and wings in 1928. Remaining in the Navy Reserve, he started Ellis Transport in 1936. Lloyd Jarman photo via Sue Bramstadt/Alaska Airlines.

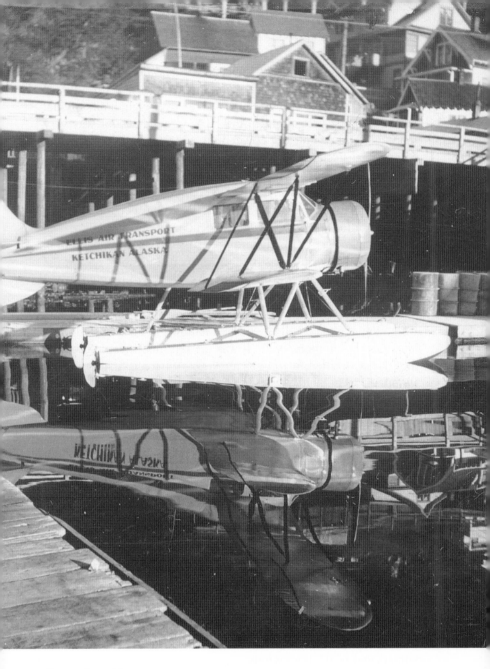

Ellis Waco in Ketchikan.

Flight training primarily consisted of dual instruction. In fact, after my four hours and forty-two minutes dual and my seventy plus solo in our Aeronca C-3, I was given over eight hours of dual before my first solo flight in the STA. Ground school was very thorough, and completely covered all subjects needed to pass the commercial license written exam. Students were required to take each license test from the CAA (the Civil Aeronautics Administration, which in 1940 was combined with the CAB, the Civil Aeronautics Board, to form the FAA, the Federal Aviation Administration). That included student pilot, private pilot, and commercial pilot. An instructor pilot test was also available. I took and passed the written instruction test part, but said "no" to the flight instructor part. I simply could not see myself returning to Juneau and ending up as a flight instructor teaching students.

In August of 1939, I passed my commercial test and left San Diego the next day. Bill Cass took me down to the bus station on his 1938 Harley motorcycle. It was the last time I would ever see him. He was killed in 1944 as an Army Air Force first lieutenant flying a DeHavilland Mosquito photo-reconnaissance fighter.

I headed for Juneau, beginning with another long bus trip to Seattle where I boarded the Alaska Steamship vessel *Yukon*. Aboard were a number of schoolteachers, and I became friends with a young lady who was going to Juneau to start her school teaching career.

Our first stop was at Metlakatla to unload cans at the fish cannery. I noticed the Ellis Air Transport Waco landing and pulling up to the float, so I walked down to talk with Bob Ellis.

I figured it would do no harm to let him know that I now had my commercial license and was looking for a job. My thoughts were that if Bob was looking for a pilot he would probably seek someone with a bit more experience, but then you never know. Ellis Air Transport was based in Ketchikan, and at the time, I looked at the Ketchikan area as a desirable place from which to fly because of its milder climate compared to Juneau with its colder winters and frigid Taku winds.

Gerald A. "Bud" Bodding. 1940.

Long-line fishing fleet at Ketchikan.

After arriving at Juneau, my next thought was employment. I dropped by Sommers Construction office and Bob Sommers advised he had a job for me and would break me in as a shovel operator. It was a good offer, but I was looking for a flying job. Mary Joyce had taken over the Gastineau Flying Club Aeronca. She allowed me to use it to take my class I-S seaplane rating test.

Both Shell Simmons of Alaska Air Transport and Alex Holden of Marine Airways had said, "Get your commercial pilot license and there will be a job for you." Now the story was, "Go out and get some experience and then there will be a job."

Alaska Air Transport and Marine Airways had merged and became Alaska Coastal Airlines. They had a surplus Fairchild 71 aircraft that they sold to Reeve Airways operating out of Valdez. There was considerable work to be done on the plane before departing Juneau, so Bob Reeve hired me as an assistant.

In the foreground, Herb Munter's Bellanca.
KEITH PETRICH PHOTO.

Bud taking off from Ketchikan's Tongass Narrows in
the WacoYKS-6.

Bud with Ellis Transport's Bellanca.

Ellis mechanic Jack Sherman, brother of Harry Sherman,
became vice president maintenance.

Herb Munter with his Ketchikan-based Bellanca Pacemaker.

Lt. Robert Ellis, USNR, and Kingfisher at Sitka. 1941.
ELLIS FAMILY PHOTO.

We finally completed the job on the Fairchild 71, and it was towed to the airport to be readied for the flight to Valdez. I approached Bob Reeve and asked him if he needed any help. He said that he was working on a Fairchild 51 in Valdez and, if I wished, I could accompany him. My pay would be room and board at his home. He stated that in the spring, if he did not have a flying job for me, he would find a job out of Anchorage, which sounded okay to me.

During this time, the schoolteacher I had met on the boat and I had been seeing each other, and I was invited to numerous school functions and parties that I was not particularly interested in. Anyhow, I figured she was not for me.

In early January 1940, we departed Juneau, stopped in Cordova for gas, and then flew on to Valdez, arriving just before dark. The Valdez airport had considerable snow and was unusable for wheel-equipped aircraft, so we landed on the mud flats. The next day, we took a pair of aircraft skis down and installed them on the 71. We then took off from the mud flats and landed on the snow-covered field.

The Reeve hangar had previously been destroyed by fire. Bob's other aircraft, the Fairchild 51, had been dismantled and was being worked on in a small heated shed. The newly acquired aircraft was tied down outside in the winter weather. Valdez is noted for its snow, and that was certainly the case when I was there. Bob Reeve and I would walk to the field daily and work on the 51.

Occasionally there would be a flight to haul supplies for prospectors and trappers. We would either drop them out the door opening from a low altitude, or sometimes land on the snow-covered glaciers and deposit our loads. In the summer after the snow had melted, prospectors would find their supplies. We would drop or land such things as sacked coal and fifty-gallon drums of gas and diesel oil. The drums were the old, heavy ones, banded with steel rims and I often wondered how many survived the drop, but the snow was really deep.

There was very little to do in Valdez in the winter. We just worked long hours. There was a movie on Friday nights, which most townspeople attended, and an occasional house party. Every time I would complain just a bit, Bob Reeve would say, "Don't forget; I saved you from the school teacher."

Tony Schwamm, owner of Petersburg Air Service. 1938.

Known as "Slim" or "Chuck," Charles Gropstis was tall: 6 ft. 6 in. He was a
native of Chicago and a veteran pilot at his death in 1941.
Lloyd Jarman photo via Marily Gropstis Chase.

On March 1, 1940, I received a letter from Bob Ellis advising that, if I was interested, he had a flying job for me in Ketchikan and to please reply. I caught Alaska Steam out of Valdez and went to work for Ellis Air Transport on March 15, 1940.

Ellis had just acquired its second aircraft. In addition to the original Waco YKS three-passenger seaplane, a five-passenger Bellanca Senior Pacemaker was added. Bob Ellis first thought he would use the second aircraft as load dictated. It soon became apparent that another pilot was needed. When I got to Ketchikan, Bob told me to take the Waco and get used to it. The CAA inspector arrived a few days later and gave me a flight test. It was not long before I was flying various trips with the Waco.

My first trip to the West Coast (western part of southeastern

Charles Gropstis and Livingstone Wernecke, July 1935, with the Bellanca Skyrocket. Wernecke was manager of the Treadwell–Yukon Mining Corp. *DELANO PHOTO VIA MARILYN GROPSTIS CHASE.*

Alaska) was with a load of Easter lilies to Craig, Klawock, and Hydaburg. I still had to gain the confidence of the locals. They were used to flying only with Bob Ellis and Herb Munter of Aircraft Charter Service.

As I recall, Bill Pries, the manager of the Annette Island Packing Company, would only fly with Bob Ellis. Pries called for a charter, Metlakatla to Hydaburg. Bob told me to take the trip. At Metlakatla, Pries came down to the float and said, "Where is Bob?" I advised that he was busy and unavailable. I noticed a little reluctance, but he got aboard and away we went to Hydaburg. On return to Metlakatla, Pries got out of the plane, turned to me, and said, "Nice ride." Gradually people got used to me and I had no further trouble. The next month I took my check ride in the Bellanca and passed okay.

After I had been working at Ellis for a couple of months, Shell Simmons had a flight to Ketchikan. He offered me $200 a month, year-round if I would go to work for him in Juneau. I told him, "No thanks." Flying jobs were getting more available. I also had an offer from Pan Am about that time; however, I was happy where I was. Then, too, my Ellis pay of $175 per month was increased by $150 a month in company stock. I became stockholder number four, along with Bob Ellis, mechanic Jack Sherman, and traffic manager Don Wright.

Days off were mainly rainy or windy ones when we chose not to fly. The Army Engineers started building an airport on Annette Island, twenty-one miles from Ketchikan, and we added another Waco seaplane to our fleet.

Dates and incidents are a bit vague, but Bob Ellis was called to active duty in the Navy in April 1941 and assigned to the Naval Air Station (NAS) in Sitka. (Many reservists like Bob were called up months before Pearl Harbor.) At the time we decided to merge our operation with Herb Munter's Aircraft Charter Service, calling our combined operation "Alaska Airlines."

Shortly after our merger, I had an incident that would have been amusing if it were not so serious. After the usual long day of flying, I had a charter with an electrician to Waterfall Cannery in Munter's Stinson. I was to wait while the electrician's job was completed.

While standing by, I noticed that the aircraft had a decided list. On investigation, I found that one float was taking on water because of a crack in the bottom of the float. Normally that would not be serious due to the floats having a number of compartments. These floats were old and brittle, however, and had numerous cracks in the bulkheads, and water was leaking between the compartments. Utilizing the hand pump, which was standard equipment, I could barely keep ahead of the incoming water. The electrician arrived, I managed to get airborne, and we were off for Ketchikan.

My main thought was to land close in to avoid excessive taxiing. On final approach, I remembered that I had forgotten to wind in my trailing antenna. That was no big deal, but I decided to go around. I reached down with my left hand, somewhat burying my head behind the instrument panel. Then I head a loud "wham." Looking out I saw a three-foot piece of a boat mast hanging from the spreader bar on the floats. We went around and this time landed really close to the hangar and ramp.

The only damage to the aircraft was a small dent on the spreader bar. We paid for replacing the mast on the fish packer *Fredrick C.* The cost was about $450. Everyone said, "Gee, you were lucky; a foot lower and you would have hit your propeller." I said, "Not so. A foot higher and I would have missed the damned thing."

At the end of the summer, we advised Munter either we would buy him out or he could buy us out. We at Ellis ended up as the owners. The purchase price was $20,000 and included one Stinson aircraft and two Bellancas. One Bellanca was in Seattle on wheels. Also included was Munter's hangar in Ketchikan. We adopted the name Ellis Air Lines (formerly Ellis Air Transport). During the latter part of September 1941, I was granted thirty days vacation, after which Herb Munter would leave the operation.

I left on the steamer *Baranof* enroute to points south with nothing particular in mind. I got together with a friend from Juneau, Rudy Pusich, who, like me, just wanted to see some sunshine. After spending a few days in Seattle, we boarded a bus and went to Los Angeles. I decided to continue on to San Diego and visit the Ryan School. Rudy stayed in Los Angeles.

There was not much of interest in California, so Rudy and I caught a bus back to Seattle where we both had friends. We checked into the New Washington Hotel and proceeded to have fun.

I received a telegram from Tony Schwamm of Petersburg Air Service, asking if I would be interested in ferrying a Waco seaplane from Seattle to Ketchikan for him. This would save me boat fare, so I jumped at the chance. The aircraft was at Boeing Field, having been converted from wheels to floats. It was trucked to the Duwamish Waterway where I picked it up and flew it over to Lake Union. I tied up at Kurtzer's Flying Service. I flew it around for a couple of days, and everything worked well. Rudy had planned on making the trip with me, but then decided he wanted to spend more time in Seattle.

What follows is an account of my attempted Seattle to Ketchikan flight in the Petersburg Air Service Waco aircraft.

III: Tragic Rendezvous

Charter a plane, fly it north from Seattle about half-way to Alaska, and you may, with a little searching, find a tiny jut of rock and timber called Salal Island. Located just off the Pacific coast of Canada's British Columbia, it is nothing more than a three-by-five-mile forest set out in the ocean. Boulder-shored and damp the year around, it is as uninviting as it is desolate. No one, to my knowledge, has ever lived there of his own choosing.

In October 1941, four of us lay stranded on its beaches, two badly injured and two already dead — victims of freak air crashes that make one of the strangest adventures in the flying history of the North.

The date was Tuesday, October 21. Young, and not then married, I had left Seattle the day before, ending a month's vacation

Bellanca 31 operated by "Slim" Gropstis at Lake Union, Seattle, Washington. *Gordon Williams photo via Donald "Bucky" Dawson.*

and returning to my Ketchikan, Alaska, pilot's job with Ellis Air Lines which, in those days, was an ambitious little bush service that was yet to become a larger, scheduled carrier.

I was flying home, delivering a single-engine Waco float plane to a friend in Alaska and saving myself the price of a steamship ticket at the same time. One passenger shared the four-seat cabin with me, a Dayton, Oregon, banker named Harry Sherman. We had met only the day before, but, cheerful and friendly, he seemed a pleasant companion to have along. He planned a short visit with Ellis Air Lines' maintenance vice president, Jack Sherman, his brother.

We departed the States at 12:30 p.m., four hours behind schedule thanks to fog and rain. Clearing Canadian customs at Vancouver, and flying on, we spent the night at Alert Bay.

We awoke on the morning of the twenty-first to overcast skies, but unlimited visibility. I called the weather station, hoping to hear we could expect the same or better all the way home. "Can't say for sure, old man," said a clipped voice at the other end of the line. "Canada's at war, you know. Weather's a bit hard to come by. But we do have one report from Prince Rupert (just across the border from Ketchikan). Two-thousand-foot ceilings and ten miles visibility."

I shrugged and told Harry we might as well take off. With weather at least fair at both ends of the line it should be okay in the middle. He nodded in agreement. "Keep your eye out for Chuck Gropstis," said the Alert Bay customs man as we left his office. "He and Livingston Wernecke are flying down from Alaska today."

"I'll do that," I said. Chuck was an old friend. He flew as personal pilot for Mr. Wernecke, who had mining interests in Alaska, northern British Columbia, and the Yukon Territory. I knew their Bellanca well and figured we would waggle wings at each other if our paths crossed on the flight.

We left at 10:00 a.m. and by 10:30 we hit our first patches of high fog. Dropping from 5,000 to 2,000 feet, to keep under the weather, we watched Vancouver Island fall away swiftly beneath our wings. Dropping more altitude, we crossed Queen Charlotte Sound, with neither the plane nor the engine giving any hint of strain.

We continued up the so-called Inside Passage between the islands and mainland of North America, and by noon, flying low, we passed the city of Bella Bella. Shortly afterwards we started across the white-capped waters of Milbanke Sound.

Now the fog really came down, only a hundred feet above the surface. Still, for visibility we had a good two miles, so we flew on.

We made it halfway across the sound before it happened. The engine, purring beautifully one moment, simply quit. No warning. No choking. No nothing.

"We're going down!" I yelled to Harry. A whisper would have been sufficient in the church-quiet cabin. If he answered, I do not know what he said. My thoughts were too busy even to be scared. Uppermost in my mind was how best to gamble the few feet of altitude we had above water.

I would land upwind, in the approved manner, and probably make a better landing. But by doing so, we would end up far from shore and out toward open ocean. Or, I could land downwind, possibly cutting in toward one of the small islands nearby. I chose the latter.

As we dropped, faster every second, I doubted my choice. Sea swells, which looked small from above, were now revealed to be twice as deep as the plane.

Suddenly, as we got really close, the bow of the floatplane thudded into one of the rock-hard mountains of water and bounced us twenty to thirty feet back into the air.

The plane stalled instantly and came over on one wing. Within a split second, amid a barrage of salt spray, broken glass, and shattering aircraft parts, we crashed and went under — upside down.

Water flooded into the cabin immediately. Dazed and shaken I kicked open the door to my left and started out. Then I looked back. Harry hung limp, anchored by his safety belt. He was unconscious and bleeding.

I reached back frantically unlatching the belt with numbed fingers, and caught him by the back of his collar. By this time, water almost filled the sinking airplane. Gulping into my lungs what seemed to be the last remaining air, I floated out and up to the surface.

The plane's pontoons, thank God, bobbed up, capsized but intact, on the water. They kept the Waco from going clear to the bottom. Choking and spewing, I grabbed one to keep us afloat. After a few minutes, I regained some strength and senses, climbing aboard the float and dragging Harry after me.

That in itself required a major effort. Harry was a big man; he would have been hard to handle even in calm waters. The terrific rise and fall of the swells made the project almost impossible. Finally, after hoisting and straining and nearly washing both of us overboard again, I got him up with me. Then I took off my belt and looped it through his. That done, I pushed it through a keel hole in the base of the float and cinched it down. For the time being at least, the unconscious Harry would not drown.

Death from his injuries was another matter, however. Across his forehead, a deep four-inch slash oozed blood constantly. I did not know from one minute to the next whether he would live or not.

I wondered if it mattered. The chilling spray and waves drenched us every second. Though born and raised in Alaska, I had never felt such cold before in my life. There was every chance, I thought, we would both die of exposure, and soon.

After perhaps half an hour, Harry came around, somewhat. Moaning through the pain, shock, and chills, he had no idea of who we were, where we were, or why we were there. But at least consciousness was returning. Then I heard another sound, far away to the north and almost drowned out by Harry's soft groan. It grew louder as it came closer. Another plane! I did not dare hope he would fly close enough to see us, yet the sounds of the engine came clearer every second. Then, through the haze, I saw it: the Gropstis–Wernecke Bellanca. The same aircraft I had planned to tip my wings to as our paths crossed to and from the north.

As soon as I saw it I waved frantically. Harry, who seemed more aware of his surroundings now, waved a little, too. Then he sat dazed again, unknowing. Closer and closer it flew, finally not more than a hundred feet above us. "Hey!" I yelled at it. "Chuck! For God's sake, Chuck! Look down!" It continued on, giving no sign of having spotted the two derelicts floating below. The engine sound faded.

Then, from the south now, the noise grew again. Perhaps they had seen us after all, and were returning to mark our location. Once more through the fog I made out the ship, but this time it flew off to one side, near an island that slowly took shape as we drifted nearer. They had not spotted us after all. Probably they had turned because of worse weather to the south. Possibly they were heading back to find a sitting-down spot, in which to wait out the fog. How I envied those lucky guys up there.

They banked still further toward the island and gradually faded from our vision. I did not see what happened next, but from the ripping, tearing thud that echoed across the waters, I knew they had cracked up at full speed somewhere on the tiny isle. From the scraping noises that continued to come back to us, it sounded as though they had crashed in timber. I turned, horrified, to Harry, who registered nothing more than the dazed expression I saw on his face before. He had heard absolutely nothing. I said little to him about it.

We drifted for a quarter hour more, slowly closing the gap between the island and us. Now Harry began to come around fast. He could talk intelligently and realized our position. Soon, with strength returning in spite of his wounds, he sat up on the float and unfastened the belt, which held him on. Then he was promptly washed overboard when a monster of a swell tipped the pontoon way over on its side.

"I'm swimming ashore!" he yelled to me. I glanced toward the island and estimated about seventy-five feet between it and our position. "You sure you can make it?" I yelled back.

He nodded and started swimming. With some misgivings I slipped into the water and paddled over to him. He seemed all right. So together we left the plane and fought the waves and swells shoreward.

The beach had me worried. Huge boulders jutted up from the water. The high, crashing, surf-breaking thunder told me the current might well dash our bodies against the rocks like so much driftwood.

Then luck, which had deserted us in the air, found us again in the water. Halfway to the beach my feet touched bottom. We had chanced upon a shallow shelf and could walk the rest of the way ashore. A few moments later we stood exhausted but thankful on almost dry land, wringing water from our clothes and talking of what we might do next.

IV: Death is a Two-sided Coin

"We'll find the Bellanca first," I said. Our first concern had to be for Chuck Gropstis and Livingston Wernecke, if they were still alive. Harry listened to my story of their crash and gave me a doubting expression. "You're sure of this Bud? You know, I'm not the only guy who's cracked his head open."

It took me a moment to realize what he meant. Then I put my hand to my forehead. I was losing as much blood as Harry! Until now, with the sea washing us every few seconds I did not even know that I had been injured. No wonder I felt so weak.

My cuts were a series of many shorter gashes, unlike Harry's one long one. My head had struck the windshield when we hit the water. Dozens of glass fragments pocked my face from the eyes up. Some cuts were deep and others were shallow. From all of them I lost blood. But, injured or not, I knew I had heard the Bellanca come down on this island. If the ship's passengers still lived, they probably needed our help.

Alive or not, they could help us. Surely they had something in the way of survival gear in the plane. If not, or if we failed to find the downed aircraft, then we faced a steady diet of beach clams, and probable death from exposure. For, as we continued to lose blood in spite of crude bandages, we felt our strength waning. I could not imagine two men in our condition living long on this chilly, windswept island, not when we lacked even matches for a fire. We started up the beach. Harry stayed near the water (because his eyesight was poor and he had lost his glasses in the Waco). I moved back into the forest. We called out to each other every few minutes, to mark our positions. Though we searched hard, neither of us found any trace of the Gropstis–Wernecke plane.

After a while Harry called out that it was getting dark. Should I not return to the beach? Discouraged, and very, very tired, I agreed and moved toward the sound of his voice. To reach him I moved down a cliff-like ravine, and at the bottom I found the wreck. I yelled and Harry hurried to me.

Together we approached the craft, or what was left of it. Actually, only the floats remained intact. I knew before we reached it that Chuck and Mr. Wernecke could not have survived. They had not. Still strapped to their seats, they hung limp and dead from the floor of the inverted cabin. They never knew what hit them.

Satisfied we could do nothing for our friends, we set about the unpleasant, but practical, task of searching the plane. We found a gold mine of supplies for shipwrecked airmen. In addition to lesser items, we hauled out two sleeping bags, a tent, a suitcase of emergency rations and equipment, cookies, a gun (with no ammunition), a bottle of rum, and a workable radio receiver.

As we organized our camp, I wondered at our phenomenally good fortune. The chances for two such near-simultaneous crashes

Coast Guard sailors inspecting the Bellanca wreckage on Salal Island.

The cutter USCGS *Cyane*, built in 1934 by Seattle-based Lake Union Drydock and Machine Works, operated out of Ketchikan, performing anti-submarine, search and rescue, and convoy escort duties during the war. Decommissioned in 1954, it passed into commercial service as a fish-processing vessel and was sunk off Mission Bay, near San Diego, in 1989 as part of an artificial reef.
PHOTO COURTESY UNITED STATES COAST GUARD HISTORICAL OFFICE.

must be one in a billion. Yet, it happened, and since it happened we saw nothing particularly unusual in the fact that six out of a dozen fresh eggs had survived the devastating crash without breaking.

I wondered, too, why we, and not the two men in the plane, had lived to now have some real hope for survival. Fate must have flipped a coin, I thought, and we won the toss. Exhausted, we slipped into our sleeping bags, after setting a splint to Harry's arm. Strangely, his wrist had been broken in the crash, but not until he started lifting gear from the Bellanca did he notice it.

The next morning I crept from the tent praying to see sun and blue skies. Instead I looked out on thicker fog than ever. Somewhat discouraged, but thankful nevertheless for our God-given bounty, we each ate a breakfast of one egg and a cookie. A limited menu, yes, but practical. Although we had rations available, they were minimal. It could be weeks — conceivably even months, if we lasted that long — before anyone found us. I was hoping for an early rescue, but I had flown the North Country much too long to count on it. Most of that first day I chopped wood for a signal fire, but had no opportunity to use it. We saw no boats or planes at all. It was not a very happy beginning.

Harry, who had spent very little time outdoors, and had never camped in the bush country, adjusted wonderfully from the beginning. His poor eyesight and broken wrist limited the work he could do, of course, but he did all he could and complained about nothing. His biggest concern was for his wife and two children. He could picture them at home in Dayton, receiving the fateful news from a telegram, "Plane overdue, presumed down at sea or along the coast."

That night, after another sparing meal, we tuned in the Vancouver newscasts on the battery-operated radio. They reported the Wernecke–Gropstis plane not yet arrived at Alert Bay, but no one seemed concerned about it. Officials assumed the aircraft lay weathered in somewhere along the coast, waiting out the fog. If anyone missed us yet, they said nothing about it.

The second day repeated the first: still foggy, still cold, still no sign of rescue. I chopped more brush, then relaxed most of the afternoon. Both of us grew weaker in spite of our food supply.

Apparently we had lost a great deal of blood. And often, as I jumped from a deadfall log, or a rock on the beach, the jolt would start my wounds bleeding again. Harry had the same experience.

That day, for the first time, we considered leaving Salal Island, which we had identified from maps in the plane. The same maps showed a lighthouse on another island thirteen miles away. We could build a raft of sorts, we figured, and try to navigate it there, inching our way through the more or less sheltered back channels. It would be risky, but at least we knew there would be people at the lighthouse. No one might ever find us on this forsaken rock.

We let the problem ride for a day. Perhaps tomorrow, if the weather cleared, we would find our position better than the maps indicated. That night the newscasters reported the Bellanca still missing.

On the third morning, we ate the last of the eggs and cursed the still-hanging fog. Finally, it began to rise at noon. At two o'clock we heard a plane. We never did see it but we lit one of our smudges anyway. The pilot did not see us either. At three o'clock another plane (or possibly the same one) flew over, this time low, quite close, and plainly visible.

We waved our hands, yelling hysterically. He simply could not miss us, not with the smudge sending columns of smoke skyward, and surely not at his low altitude. But he did and flew on. We both felt sick to our stomachs. So near. Late in the afternoon, we saw a few boats, far out to sea. But they too ignored the smoke signals we burned continuously now.

Believe me, it actually makes you physically ill, being trapped that way, watching help appear on the horizon, only to see it ignore your most frantic efforts. Two men never felt lower.

The fourth day dawned clearer and warmer, but our spirits, with our strength, continued to fall. Harry worried more and more about his family. I knew my folks in Juneau would be sick with anxiety.

Later that day the steamship *North Sea* came fairly close, but it too passed us by. Ironically, the twisted hull of that big liner now lies rusting on the rocks of those very waters.

During the day, I again collected firewood and brush. That

night we made a decision; if help did not come the next morning we would start building our raft.

For the first time the nightly news reported our plane overdue. "All hope has now been abandoned for the also-missing Gropstis–Wernecke plane," said the announcer. "There is some talk among officials that this aircraft may have collided in midair with the Bodding–Sherman Waco."

Awake in my sleeping bag long after the newscast ended, I thought of the two poor devils back in the woods. They had not done it on purpose, of course, but they had given their lives that we might live. I wondered if their sacrifice had been in vain.

Tomorrow the fires would be bigger than ever. And if, Lord willing, someone saw them and took us off this open-air prison I would try to make Chuck's and Mr. Wernecke's deaths something more than a heads-we-won toss-up. Maybe I had been wrong earlier. Perhaps death is not a two-sided coin. Maybe it is many-sided. Maybe their two deaths could save many, many lives.

For a youth of twenty-four, I became awfully philosophical that night, but in the years since, I have tried to keep those thoughts in mind. And as vice president-chief pilot for Ellis Air Lines, I like to think that our twenty-five million scheduled passenger miles of death-free flying had something to do with those two crashes back on Salal Island. I like to think my experience there made a better pilot of me, one more cautious and respectful of weather and the elements and that my standards have affected our other pilots too.

When we woke that fifth morning on the island, I postponed worry about flying standards. My big concern was signal fires. We got a big one going, and then I wandered up the beach, searching the air and water with binoculars taken from the Bellanca.

Using the glasses, I spotted the boat first — a small Canadian patrol craft, paralleling the shore. I held my breath, hoping and hoping. Then it blew its whistle, long and shrill and beautiful. "Harry!" I yelled back. "Harry! Did you hear that?"

He came running. "What was it? A boat?" I pointed to the ever-growing ship out in the water. Soon it passed us and went out of sight. Harry sighed, despairingly, but I felt sure we had been spotted. "There's a rock ledge between him and us," I said. "I think he doubled around, to come back inside the breakers." And that was exactly what happened.

Within an hour, the boat returned and sent a skiff through the surf to bring us aboard. Harry's eyes dampened as he leaped into the shore boat. Personally, I could have kissed the guy that steered it to us.

Aboard the vessel (and eating the world's tastiest beef roast), I recounted our experience to the skipper, Vic Bond. He listened, incredulous, to our story of two simultaneous crashes in such deserted, frontier country.

"We owe everything, our lives included, to those fellows back there," I told him, finishing the tale. "We've lived, literally, in dead men's shoes. We've slept in their tent, and we've eaten their food for the past five days."

"The way I figure it," I said, "the only thing we did for ourselves, the only thing we don't owe to them, is this rescue."

"You owe them for that, too," said the captain, very softly. "We weren't looking for you. We were searching for Gropstis and Wernecke."

After being rescued from Salal Island by the Canadian police patrol boat, skipper Vic Bond, and crewman Doug Gory, we were taken to Klem Tu, a small cannery village where a nurse took care of Harry Sherman's broken wrist and our head wounds.

The next morning the USCG cutter *Cyane* arrived. We were taken aboard and returned to the accident scene. The bodies of Wernecke and Gropstis were taken from the wreckage. I observed the metal frame of the Waco on the rocky beach. All the fabric had been stripped by the waves. The floats were nowhere to be seen, nor the wing panels. Our next stop was at Prince Rupert, British Columbia, where I testified at the inquest on the deaths of Gropstis and Wernecke.

Married, and with two young daughters back home in Oakland, California, Chuck Gropstis was an exceptional pilot with nearly 5,000 hours in his logbooks. He had flown in the Caribbean and Latin America in addition to Alaska, where he was a contemporary of Bob Ellis when they both flew for Pan Am's subsidiary, Pacific Alaska Airways in the mid 1930s. At the time of his death, he was flying for Treadwell–Yukon again, only on a temporary basis, having been granted a short leave of absence from his employer, Consolidated Aircraft of San Diego. Earlier in 1941, he had joined Consolidated as a ferry pilot, flying the big, new B-24 Liberator bombers from San Diego to the east coast where other crews ferried them across the Atlantic for service with the Royal Air Force.

The next day we arrived in Ketchikan, and I visited Dr. Cramer. He took one look at my head wounds and advised his receptionist that he would be busy for the rest of the day. He removed a number of pieces of glass, did a bit of cutting, and then finished with a dozen or so stitches. I took a few more days off and then returned to flying, at which time Herb Munter departed.

The military draft had been instituted, but due to my flying job, I had no trouble getting a deferment. I did have to report monthly to the local draft board, however. The Navy was short on utility aircraft, and they soon commandeered four of our aircraft: two Wacos, a Bellanca, and a Stinson, together with a hangar we had purchased from Munter.

That left us with two operating aircraft, plus the Bellanca on wheels in Seattle. Arnold Enge, Hugh Ramsdell, and I were the remaining pilots. Business was not that great, gas was in short supply, and travel was limited. Arnold Enge served as a civilian pilot flying the Navy-acquired Waco on patrol out over Dixon Entrance.

PART TWO:

V: Naval Aviation Volunteer

I had the day off on December 7, 1941, Pearl Harbor Day, and was sleeping in. At the time I was living in a small Ketchikan apartment located above what became Tongass Ladies' and Men's Wear. My dad was in town visiting, but due to the small size of my apartment, he was staying around the corner at the Ingersoll Hotel. There was a knock on my door, and it was my dad with the news, "Pearl Harbor has been bombed by the Japs."

Bob Ellis, being in the Naval Reserve, had previously been called to active duty and was stationed at NAS Sitka as a lieutenant. In those days, I made occasional trips to Sitka and would lunch with Bob. Through him I became acquainted with the skipper of the air station.

On one of my visits, Captain Tate asked if I would be interested in applying for a commission in the U.S. Navy. Up to this time, as stated previously, I had no problem with the draft board. Then too, being young, single, and interested in the Navy, I jumped at the chance. Captain Tate said he would get the paper work started immediately.

He stated that the Navy was very interested in pilots with Alaskan flying experience. At the time, I had well over 1,600 hours of Alaskan flying. I received numerous forms to complete, after which, I was directed to go to the nearest naval air station for a physical exam. At NAS Sitka, the dentist advised I would not qualify because I did not have the required number of teeth. I told him to call Captain Tate, and the captain's answer was, "Get him a waiver! He's going out to fight Japs, not bite them." I was also concerned about my vision check, but beat that by memorizing the 20/20 line on the chart when the examiner was out of the room.

Lt. Bob Ellis on Navy Reserve duty in 1938.

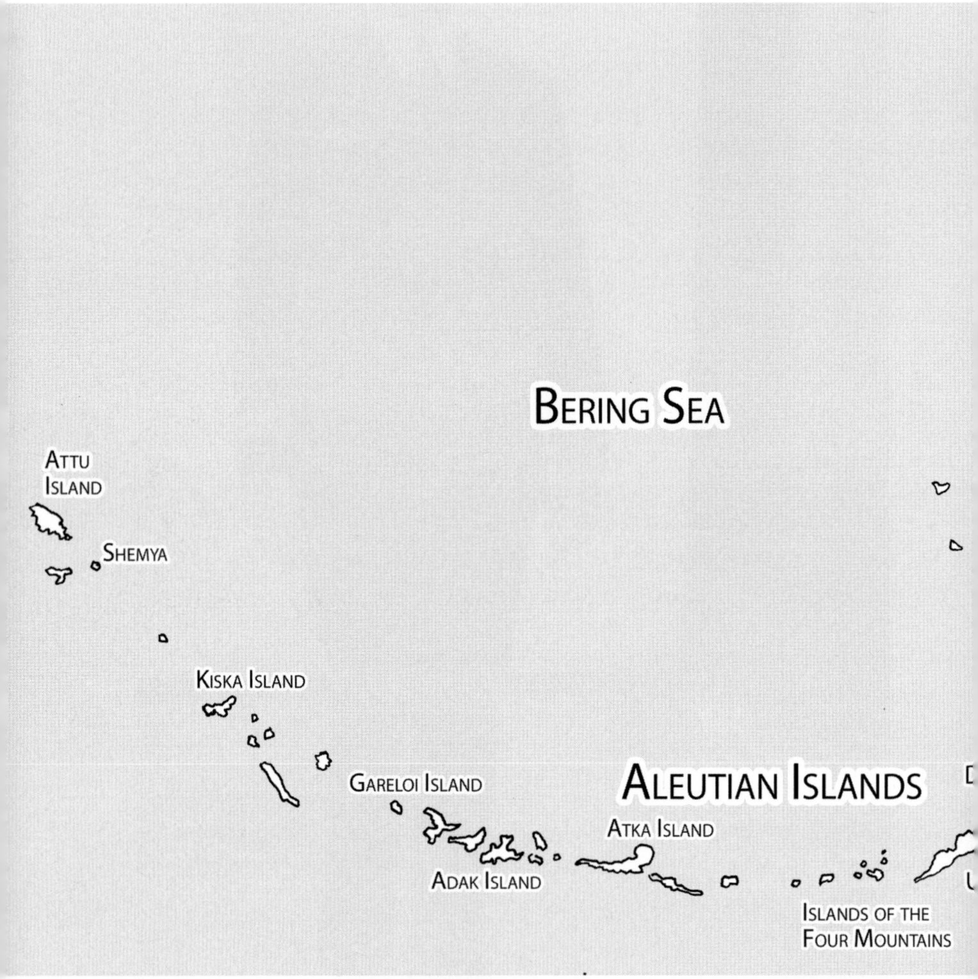

BERING SEA

ATTU
ISLAND

SHEMYA

KISKA ISLAND

GARELOI ISLAND

ALEUTIAN ISLANDS

ATKA ISLAND

ADAK ISLAND

ISLANDS OF THE
FOUR MOUNTAINS

ALASKA

Anchorage

Kodiak

KODIAK ISLAND

Cold Bay

Sand Point

rbor

UNALASKA ISLAND

AND

Charcoal portrait of Bud in uniform in 1944.

On May 19, 1942, I was commissioned as an ensign and was sworn into the Navy by the U.S. Coast Guard in Ketchikan, and shortly thereafter I received orders to report to NAS Kodiak for active duty. My problem was getting to Kodiak. I figured my best bet was to go to Sitka where PBY aircraft might stop en route Seattle/Kodiak. I waited around a week with no luck. Tony Schwamm, formerly of Petersburg Air Service and a Navy reserve officer, had been called to active duty and was commanding officer at the Navy section base at Port Althorp, about fifty or so miles northwest of Sitka. He had his own Taylorcraft seaplane stored in a hangar at NAS Sitka. He advised me that if I would fly the Taylorcraft to Port Althorp, he would take me to Juneau.

At the Baranof Hotel, I contacted Art Woodley of Woodley Airlines who had a Stinson Tri-Motor and was leaving for Anchorage the next morning. Art said that if I were at the Juneau airport at 8:00 a.m. he would take me to Anchorage and see that I got to Kodiak from there.

The next morning, I found Art waiting for me. He had six drums of aviation gas, which he needed help getting aboard. We then flew to Yakutat where we unloaded the drums. Apparently, aviation gas was in short supply and Art was storing it for future use.

While we were there, a Navy Grumman Goose taxied up and I went over and introduced myself to the pilot, Lt. Dawson. He was en route to Sitka, then returning to Kodiak. He suggested I accompany him to Sitka and then to Kodiak, so about a week later I was back where I started. The next day we left Sitka, overnighted in Cordova, and arrived at Kodiak on July 4, 1942. I was then told to report to the medical officer for another physical. This time I did not get a look at the eye chart and could not pass the vision test. The doctor, however, said he would see about getting a waiver. Within a week I had the waiver and glasses, which I would be required to wear while piloting aircraft.

Next came my checkout in Navy aircraft, beginning with the Grumman J2F Duck, a biplane amphibian. Pilot "Jenx" Jenkins took me out and rode through two water takeoffs and landings. Then the next day, I was assigned a trip to Cordova to pick up a Lt.

Introduced in 1937 as a commercial amphibian, the Grumman model G21-A went into naval service two years later as the JRF Goose. *U.S. NATIONAL ARCHIVES.*

Kingfisher from Scouting Squadron 70 hauled up the ramp on Kodiak. *ELLIS FAMILY PHOTO.*

Erskine. The weather was lousy, and I rather wondered if I would make it. This was in a strange aircraft and in a strange area. When I arrived at Cordova, I decided to try a wheel landing at the airport. Wind conditions were good and my first wheel landing in the Duck was okay. The flight back to Kodiak was without incident, and I made a water landing.

The J2F was a bit cranky on wheel landings, but water landings were something else. The Duck was not an easy seaplane to land by usual means because it was nose-heavy. The only way to make a safe landing was to level off about ten feet high and then "drop" the plane in, i.e., deliberately stall it out and let it fall the remaining few feet onto the water's surface. While in Kodiak, I witnessed two attempts of "burn on" landings (nearly perfect level landings, used with most seaplanes) with the Duck; both ended in "water loops" in which the planes hooked a wing float and then turned over on their backs.

Bob Ellis commanded Scouting Squadron 70 on Kodiak in 1942.
ELLIS FAMILY PHOTO.

Then the time came for me to be checked out in the twin-engine Grumman Goose (JRF). I was assigned as copilot with a Lt. Elliott on a flight to Sand Point, Cold Bay, and return to Kodiak. The next day I was assigned as pilot on a similar trip, without a copilot.

Sometime later I had Admiral Carl Trexel, a "CB" (Construction Battalion "Seabee"), aboard headed out to Sand Point in the JRF Goose. Weather was good at Kodiak on departure, and was reported "good" at Sand Point, which was also known as Unga. About an hour out of Kodiak, I could see weather ahead, so elected to go above it at about 5,000 feet. One problem though — the top kept getting higher, and the heavily loaded aircraft would not climb any higher. I started getting into the clouds, and shortly after, solid clouds. Then ice started forming, making it a heavier airplane. With my instrument-flying experience at a minimum, I throttled back and started a spiral down. We broke out at the 1,000-foot level and continued to Sand Point. When we pulled out on the

The Grumman J2F Duck was employed by the Navy as a general purpose scout, rescue, and target tug amphibian. *U.S. NATIONAL ARCHIVES.*

ramp, the Admiral got out and remarked, "I haven't smoked for three years. Does anyone have a cigarette?"

After the war was over and I had returned to Ellis, I was at Annette Island airfield and noticed Admiral Trexel coming off a Navy plane. I walked over and talked to him, and noticed he immediately lit up a cigarette. I remarked, "Admiral, I see you are still smoking." He answered, "Yes, thanks to you."

It could have been worse; what if there had been a 100-foot ceiling under the overcast?

For a period of time I alternated flying the JRF and the J2F. On some of the J2F flights, we would fly out to sea and tow target sleeves for destroyers and cruisers to shoot at. The J2F was equipped with a removable hatch through which the sleeve, attached to a cable, would be strung. There was at least a thousand feet of cable on a reel in the lower compartment. A mechanic would be the one to string the sleeve. Sometimes the sleeve would be completely shot away; at other times, there were no hits. Every seventh shot was a tracer bullet, so the gunners knew where their shots were going.

We were also assigned to tracking flights for the Army and Navy gunnery emplacements. They would use live ammunition and aim directly at the plane, but airbursts were supposed to be in back of the plane. However, there were no special precautions, so I often hoped that they were not too trigger-happy.

Besides the twice-weekly flights to Sand Point/Cold Bay, another regular trip was to a Navy rest camp at Afognak Lake on Afognak Island. It was a nice fishing spot and was overrun with rabbits. We had a few good rabbit feeds after trips to Afognak.

For wartime service, NAS Kodiak was not bad. Even as a junior officer, I was quartered in a fourplex unit with three other officers. There were four bedrooms, four bathrooms, kitchen, dining room, living room with a fireplace, deep shag rugs, and nice furniture, etc. Our rooms were made up daily and the entire unit kept clean. If we wished, we could cook our own meals with food from the well-stocked commissary; or the other option was to dine at the officer's mess across the street where the tables were set with white linen, napkins, and nice dishes. If you didn't like the meal for the

Grumman JRF Goose at Cold Bay, Alaska. January 12, 1943.
U.S. National Archives.

day, you could put a quarter on your plate and get a steak cooked to order.

The mail flight to Sand Point and Cold Bay was not a popular trip because the weather was seldom desirable. One time after I had flown two successive trips on that route, the second in very lousy weather, I saw on the flight board that I was again scheduled for that flight. That evening I approached the operations officer, Lt. Cdr. Rice and told him I was a bit "put out" being scheduled for a third trip to Cold Bay while the rest of the pilots took the local trips.

He said, "Okay, I have just the trip for you. Admiral John Reeves, COMALSEC, has just acquired a PBY-5A aircraft, and we want to check out an operations crew on it. Tomorrow morning, the Admiral is going to Sitka and you can go along. Possibly you can get some flight control time."

I ended up riding in the navigator's compartment. We stayed in Sitka for a couple of days and then the Admiral advised that he wanted to go to Seattle. I thought that was great, contemplating a few liberty days before returning to Kodiak.

The next morning we taxied down the ramp at Sitka for our water takeoff. The plane was heavily loaded with gas, and the pilot made two attempts before getting airborne. The weather was not

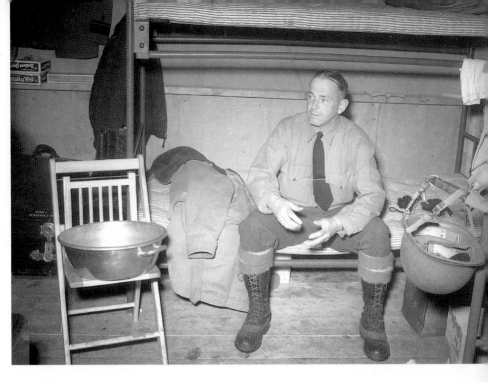

Admiral John Reeves in an informal moment on Adak. June 11, 1943.
U.S. National Archives.

too good as we proceeded down the coast to the vicinity of Cape Muzon.

On the interphone I heard the pilot calling the Admiral, who was in the blister compartment, suggesting that we divert to the Annette Island Airport and await better weather. I didn't think that the weather was too bad for the type of flying we were doing. Then too, my thoughts were that if we went to Annette, the Admiral would get aboard a Navy Air Transport aircraft, and we would go right back to Kodiak. I walked back to the blister compartment and the Admiral said to me, "Bodding, you know this area, what would you do if you were flying this aircraft?"

I answered, "I would proceed outside of the Queen Charlotte Islands and take a look before going to Annette." "Good idea," the Admiral said. He passed the word on to the pilot, and we continued. Thirty minutes later, we broke out into sunshine.

The PBY Catalina was produced in both seaplane and amphibian versions. Its range approached 2,400 miles. *U.S. National Archives.*

Having a fire extinguisher at the ready was on the starting checklist for all great round engines, a pair Pratt & Whitney 1200 hp Wasps in the Catalina's case. *U.S. National Archives.*

As a patrol bomber, the PBY Catalina could carry up to 4,000 pounds of bombs.
U.S. NATIONAL ARCHIVES.

The Consolidated PBY Catalina entered service in the 1930s and served as the Navy's standard long-range patrol bomber during World War Two. *U.S. NATIONAL ARCHIVES.*

The Lockheed Lodestar was originally developed for airline use and traced its origins to the Lockheed Electra series of twin-engine transport aircraft.
U.S. NATIONAL ARCHIVES.

Due to the short days of December, it was beginning to get dark when we passed Port Angeles. The pilot decided to land at the Coast Guard air station there. The Coast Guard then flew the Admiral in a Grumman JRF to NAS Sand Point. We spent the night at Port Angeles and flew to Seattle the next day.

Our orders were to remain until the Admiral's new Lockheed R5O Lodestar arrived from the factory. While at Sand Point, I had the occasion to go on a test hop in the PBY and got to make a wheel landing with it. On December 24, the Admiral's Lodestar arrived and early on Christmas Day, we left in the PBY and arrived at Kodiak late that evening.

Shortly thereafter, the PBY made another flight to Seattle. Lt. Herb White made the trip. He got to make one water landing. The next morning, after the PBY returned to Kodiak, the flight board showed White and Bodding assigned to the PBY to check radar beacons. I like to say, that White checked me out on water landings and I checked him out on wheels. White and I continued to fly the PBY and were still attached to operations Kodiak. I stayed in con-

The North American Texan served as an advanced trainer and general purpose aircraft as the SNJ in the Navy or the AT-6 in the Army Air Force. *U.S. NATIONAL ARCHIVES.*

The Japanese were not the only enemy in the North Pacific. The weather was a formidable foe, too. Adak, February 17, 1943. *U.S. NATIONAL ARCHIVES.*

tact with Herb White, who eventually moved to Florida. We'd get on the phone and talk about the old Navy days.

On June 9, 1943, Herb White and I were assigned to staff COMALSEC (Commander Alaska Section) and moved with the staff to NAS Dutch Harbor. At the time, the Admiral's fleet of aircraft consisted of his personal plane, the Lockheed Lodestar, the PBY, and the Grumman JRF. During my duty time at Dutch Harbor, I alternated between flying the PBY with White and flying the JRF.

On June 16, 1943, I received written orders to act as an escort in JRF 6449 to two Kingfishers on floats and an SNJ on wheels from Dutch Harbor to Adak. The orders were very specific, and somewhat ridiculous, "In case a plane is forced down and lands in the water, the JRF will land and recover the pilot and passengers. In the case of the floatplanes do all practicable to secure the plane for possible salvage. In the case of the SNJ, demolish the plane to ensure it sinks. During all this time, the remaining planes will circle and wait."

These orders were signed by R.D. Hogle, COMALSEC Ops officer (a pilot) who should have known better. The spots along the chain between Dutch Harbor and Adak where a safe water landing could be made were very limited.

Our departure from Dutch Harbor was delayed for a number of days on account of weather. During our wait, we were joined by a second SNJ piloted by Lt. "Buster" Hoyle. We finally got started in weather reported "just fair" enroute, and continued past Umnak Island. A bit more than an hour out, Lt. Hoyle kept getting out of formation and finally disappeared. The rest of us turned around and returned to Dutch Harbor where we received word that the missing SNJ had landed on the field at Atka. Later on I learned that Lt. Hoyle had gotten stuck in the overcast and then pulled up on top. Lucky for him, there was a hole over Atka, and he got down on the field okay.

The next day we made another try for Adak and arrived without incident. My orders then were to remain at Adak where the Admiral was moving headquarters. Lt. White and the PBY also arrived at Adak.

At the time, the field at Adak was Army controlled. It had been built in record time by draining a lake and laying steel mat over the two runways. Housing was in tents, with a large tent for a mess hall. A bunch of us pilots got together and assembled a Quonset hut. That work was done in less than two days, and Lt. White, six other pilots, and I moved into it.

Soon after we moved into the hut, two Coast Guard pilots with a PBY aircraft en route to Attu moved in with us while awaiting fair weather. They would not divulge the purpose of their trip, but their cargo was top secret. After a few days they finally departed, but did not get very far. They crashed on a mountain next to the field, and the two pilots and their four passengers were killed. When weather cleared enough we could see the wreckage from our Quonset hut. The next day we buried all six on the Adak "Boot Hill."

Sometime later the skipper of NAS Adak moved out of his quarters. It remained empty for a while, so Lt. White, other operations officers, and I moved in. Nobody objected.

Admiral Reeves did not get along too well with the Army in Adak so he decided to build his own airport at the Andrew Lagoon area. It was winter and a Navy Seabee detachment arrived to construct the field, hangars, and Navy quarters. The Seabees were told that on completion of the construction they would be rotated to the "Lower 48." There was a lot of mud to be moved and hills to be leveled. The ground was frozen, which made it easier to handle. It was smoothed over, and steel mat was placed for the runway.

In July 1943, they "turned the crank" and I was promoted from ensign to lieutenant (JG). Shortly after, A Grumman JRF cracked up out of Sitka, killing all on board and I received orders to ferry Grumman Bureau No.6449, which was being reassigned from COMALSEC Adak to NAS Kodiak. Kodiak's Grumman No.6448 was assigned to Sitka as a replacement.

I had some important "hand-carry" papers for Admiral Reeves, who was waiting in Kodiak for them. On delivery of the papers, the Admiral advised me that he was issuing orders for me to deliver Grumman 6448 to Sitka, and that I was to remain there as a pilot of that aircraft pending replacement of his JRF 6449. Lt. Buster Hoyle had been assigned to the Sitka duty and was a bit put out when his orders were cancelled.

Lockheed Lodestar at Adak. 1943.

Navy base at Adak. 1944.

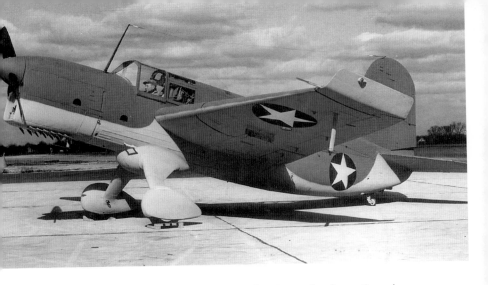

The Curtiss SOC3C was produced in both land and seaplane versions for scouting and observation, but was withdrawn from service before the war ended. *U.S. National Archives.*

Duty at Sitka was great after the Aleutians. Lt. Coligny, Sitka Station Manager, interpreted my orders as written, and the only plane I was flying was the JRF. Other station aircraft included a Curtiss SO3C Seagull, an SNJ Texan on wheels, a Grumman J4F Widgeon, and a Vought OS2U Kingfisher on floats. Originally there had been two SNJ aircraft assigned to NAS Sitka, the other one piloted by former Ellis pilot, Ensign Arnold Enge. On departure from Juneau to Sitka, Enge was flying out just behind the other SNJ. I never heard exactly what happened, but he apparently stalled out and dived straight into the mud flats. Arnold was killed instantly.

Lt Coligny had a medical problem and was replaced by Lt. Harden. Right off, he called a meeting of all OPS pilots and he said to me, "Bodding, you've been riding the gravy train long enough. From now on everyone flies the JRF, and you can fly the other aircraft as well."

NAS Sitka did not have a landing field, but there was a paved area about 800 feet long with arresting gear at one end. It was experimental, and had only been used once on the arrival of the SNJ. The other wheel plane, the SO3C had been dropped off by a Navy ship.

Although also produced in a landplane version, the Vought OS2U Kingfisher is best remembered as a scout/observation seaplane. *U.S. NATIONAL ARCHIVES.*

Powered by a pair of 200-hp Ranger in-line engines, the Grumman J4F-2 went into service with the Navy in 1942. *U.S. NATIONAL ARCHIVES.*

Tests were set up for the arresting gear, and the commanding officer at NAS Sitka, Commander Taylor, chose to make the flights. First was the SO3C. The takeoff was okay, but then came the landing. Taylor completely missed the arresting gear, ran out of landing area, turned up a road, ground looped, and collapsed the landing gear.

He was not satisfied with that, so next he tried the SNJ. Again he missed the arresting gear, landed, stomped on the brakes, and ended up on his nose, damaging the prop, engine, and cowling.

A few days later, Taylor took the JRF on a flight to Annette Island. While taxiing out at Annette, he ground looped, wiping out the landing gear and doing severe damage to the hull. That evening Lt. Harden asked me, "Did you hear what happened to your airplane?" I said, "Yes, you can notify the Admiral."

By this time I had been flying the rest of the station aircraft, mostly the Grumman Widgeon. I had been spoiled flying the JRF and did not enjoy flying the Widgeon. One of our jobs was sleeve towing and tracking in the OS2U for the Army. This was no fun either. On training missions, we would spend as long as two hours making figure eights over gun emplacements. For sleeve towing, the cable was short. On one occasion, Lt. Tom Case was towing and got a bullet through his wing tank. Two feet to the right and he would have been hit. That ended our towing flights.

On September 27, 1943, Lt. Tom Case told me that he had received orders to report to NAS Adak for duty and we speculated that possibly he would replace me at Adak. Later that day, however, I also received orders, "Proceed via government aircraft to Seattle, Washington. Upon arrival, report as instructed verbally for temporary duty in accordance with a dispatch from the commander Alaskan Sector which cannot be quoted herein. Class 1 air priority authorized." Verbally I was advised that I had been named as prospective pilot to relieve Lt. Dawson as pilot of the Admiral's Lodestar. There were no flights between Sitka and Seattle, so Lt. Case and I were put aboard a utility boat that night for Juneau.

At Juneau, I was rushed to the airport, got on a Pan Am Navy contract aircraft, and flew on to Seattle. Arriving at Boeing Field, I was paged and told to immediately call Lt. Dawson, the admiral's pilot. That call ended my hopes of spending a week or so getting checked out. Dawson said, "I'm glad you are here. We are leaving for Adak in the morning. Will see you at NAS Sand Point at 7:00 a.m."

Apparently Dawson wasn't in a hurry to leave either. We taxied out to the runway and on run up the right engine spit and popped. (The type of engine on the Lodestar was noted for fouled spark plugs when idled too long.) We taxied back to the hangar and Dawson told the crew, "Change that right engine." That at least gave mea couple more nights in Seattle.

We finally left Seattle, overnighted in Kodiak, and then flew on to Adak. So far, there had been no flying from the left seat for me. At Adak, Dawson took me out to shoot some landings. We had a propeller run away on the first takeoff, and I went around and made the landing. The next day, we took off for Kodiak. When we arrived, Dawson said, "It's your airplane. I'm gone." I was assigned a copilot, CAP Allen (Chief, Aviation Pilot, a chief petty officer with a pilot rating).

Up to this time my instrument flight time was practically nil. Back in 1939, I had ten hours under the hood at the Ryan School. Then too, I had busted through a few clouds on flights down the chain

During WWII the Navy used Lockheed R5Os for both troop and executive transport. In addition to crew, the R5O could carry 14 passengers. *U.S. NATIONAL ARCHIVES.*

in the JRF. During my duty days at NAS Kodiak, I did get thirty-two hours in a Link trainer (the first flight simulator, used for instrument flight training). Nevertheless, my instructor, Chief Hubbard, presented me with an instrument card on which was written, "Corresponds to senior pilot Army." We departed Kodiak for Adak in the Lodestar via Dutch Harbor with a load of high-ranking officers.

I climbed to cruising altitude and put the plane on automatic pilot. We were in the overcast and started picking up ice. The wing de-icer boots seemed to handle it okay, but the propeller de-icer fluid was not. Nobody had briefed me on when to use the de-icer boots or to use alcohol on the props. With the de-icer fluid on, pieces of ice were being dislodged and banging against the side of the fuselage. The remaining ice on the props caused them to get out of balance. Soon the instrument panel was shaking like it would tear loose.

I took the plane off automatic pilot, made a 180-degree turn, dropped down a thousand feet, and returned to Kodiak. I learned my lesson: turn the prop de-icer fluid on as soon as ice is suspected. The next day, I filed my clearance for 500 feet on top. We arrived at Dutch Harbor and Adak without incident.

Navy field on Attu. 1944.

On Attu, a PBY Catalina and OS2U Kingfisher about to launch for patrol.
U.S. NATIONAL ARCHIVES.

Attu. 1944.

I gradually broke in on instrument flying and learned the "dos and don'ts." Most of the time in the Aleutians, a 500-foot on top clearance would work. Then the only problem would be getting down through the overcast at the destination. The instruments on the Lodestar were the best available at the time, including dual radio altimeters, dual automatic direction finders, and radar.

The radar was read by the radioman sitting behind the bulkhead on the copilot's side. He would read the "blips" and relay distances to me via interphone. This helped some when approaching places like Dutch Harbor. Mostly I relied on the dual automatic direction finders and radio altimeters in conjunction with radio ranges on approaches and let downs.

Admiral Reeves was a rather tough old geezer, but I had no problems with him. My first trip with him aboard the Lodestar was scheduled from Adak to Attu. The weather was fair at Adak. Attu weather was reported zero–zero with fog. Shemya, the next landing field to Attu was also reporting fog. I called the Admiral and suggested we hold for weather improvement. He said, "Let's go and take a look at it." We did, getting thirty minutes out of Attu with no improvement. I advised the Admiral that we were returning to Adak. He said, "You are flying the airplane." The next day the weather opened up and we made Attu okay, spending a couple of days there.

During our stay, Jap aircraft bombed us. It was during lunchtime, and I was sitting in the mess hall when we heard a number of loud blasts. We all immediately evacuated the building and jumped into a ditch along side. We were in mud up to our knees. All the bombs fell up in the bay and nothing was damaged. Fighter planes were scrambled from Shemya, but did not intercept the bombers.

Shortly after the Attu trip, Admiral Whiting replaced Admiral Reeves as COMALSEC. He was a mild-mannered person and was not too happy about the Lodestar. Apparently, he had a brother who had been killed in a plane crash. On one occasion he went to Attu on board the gunboat *Charleston*. I had orders to follow with the Lodestar, but finding he had departed Attu, returned to Adak.

On another occasion, Admiral Whiting called me into his office and advised me that I was to put fifty hours a month on the aircraft; apparently he was afraid of losing the plane if it could not be utilized sufficiently. He stated that his chief of staff, Captain McKinnon, was going home to Juneau for Christmas and I was to fly him there and bring him back after New Years. The aircraft was at my disposal while waiting at Juneau, so I took the liberty of flying it to Ketchikan via Annette Island.

During Admiral Whiting's tour of duty, I did fly him on a few trips up and down the chain, to Seattle, and twice to Washington, DC. There were a number of flights up and down the chain with his staff members. I rarely had trouble getting my required fifty hours per month.

On one particular flight to Kodiak, with weather at minimums, I was making my approach and saw no reason for not using all of my electrical instruments including radar. On my way down, every electrical circuit went out leaving just my basic instruments and no radio. I immediately pulled up and returned on top. After shutting the radar off, we had power to run everything else. On our next approach, we got in at Kodiak without the help of radar. A few days later we were on our way to Seattle to have larger capacity batteries and generators installed.

The Lodestar was painted in the Navy's blue camouflage col-

Adm. Francis E. Whiting. *U.S. NATIONAL ARCHIVES.*

ors. An order came out that transport type aircraft could have the paint removed. Since the camouflage paint on a large plane cost us five to ten miles of airspeed, I had no trouble convincing the Admiral that the removal should be done.

On another trip to Seattle, on April 15, 1944, I received orders detaching me from duty with staff COMALSEC. I was to report to the commandant of the Seventeenth Naval District as a member of his staff. This was merely a paper change as far as I was concerned. COMALSEC was under the Thirteenth Naval District with headquarters in Seattle. Alaska then became a district of its own as the Seventeenth Naval District.

VI: Flying the Brass

I was happy with my job in the Navy flying the Aleutians with trips to the Lower 48. The way I looked at it, if I were to transfer, the best I could hope for was some utility flying job. Then too, I was pretty much in my own backyard and was drawing overseas pay. Normally, duty time overseas was limited to one year.

At one time, Lt. Cdr. Crawshaw was assigned to COM 17 (Commander 17th Naval District) staff. It was believed that he was to take over my job, and I would be receiving orders. He pretty well let it be known he was senior to me and would be taking over as the Admiral's pilot. Apparently, the Admiral did not concur. Crawshaw ended up with a desk job.

While traveling to various military bases with brass aboard, especially the Admiral, there were numerous parties, and I usually had an invitation. Once at Elmendorf Army Air Base at Anchorage, we were invited to a party at a general's quarters. The apartment was nice, but there was nothing in the way of furniture, except rustic tables, folding chairs, and a piano which made me realize how well off and lucky I was to be in the Navy.

On an overnight in Kodiak I attended a party at the CO's quarters. It was a beautiful, well-furnished house. I was introduced to a number of civilians, including a Miss O'Driscoll and a Mister Flynn. It took a while for that to sink in. They were Martha O'Driscoll and Errol Flynn of movie fame.

On one interesting flight out of Adak, I flew the first eight Navy nurses to be assigned to NAS Attu after the Japs were cleaned out. They were the first women on the island and were afforded quite a welcome. When exceptional USO troops were in Adak, the Admiral would entertain them. Then I would fly them to Attu and return, thus meeting a number of interesting people in the process.

When I received my commission as an ensign, I had a designation as AVP, meaning Aviation Volunteer Probationary. Admiral Whiting took it upon himself to get that changed. On May 5, 1944, the following message was sent from COM 17 to Navy Bureau of Personnel, "Request reserve classification in the case of Lt. (JG) Alfred Gerald Bodding be changed from Aviation Volunteer Probationary to Aviation Volunteer Transport. Bodding's comprehensive knowledge of flying conditions in Alaska in my opinion makes him one of the outstanding pilots in the district." That's all it took. All AVT designations were later changed to A5L.

On most flights I was issued orders that were hard to decipher. In May 1944 I had orders to proceed via government or commercial air from Adak to Dutch Harbor, Kodiak, Anchorage, Sitka, and Juneau in connection with the decommissioning of the NAS Sitka.

Actually, my orders meant I was to take the Lodestar from Adak to Juneau, picking up officer personnel en route. Since there was no landing field in Sitka, my passengers would get there from Juneau by other means. I would wait in Juneau and then take my passengers back to their various stations. I do not know why orders were written as they were, except if the enemy got their hands on them, they would not know what was going on. Most orders were confusing, but then I had verbal orders also.

The crew on the Lodestar consisted of the pilot, a copilot, a radioman who also operated the radar, a chief aviation machinist, and an orderly. We had ten other plush seats. The plane was nice to

Hiking party on Attu. 1945. L to R: Lt. Wilson, Cmdr. Ellis, Lt. Bodding.
ELLIS FAMILY PHOTO.

fly and fast for its day. Occasionally, we would be holding at Dutch Harbor with Naval Air Transport R4Ds. I could lounge around until I heard the R4Ds depart and would beat them to Adak.

On June 24, 1944, I had a flight to Washington, DC. My orders were to report on arrival to the Commanding Officer, NAS Anacostia. My verbal orders were to take Admiral Whiting and other staff members to Washington, and when they finished their business return them to Adak. It was a nice trip with overnight stops at Anchorage, Edmonton, Minneapolis, and then on to Washington.

My crew and I found Minneapolis to be a great liberty town because they rarely saw Navy personnel. On subsequent trips, I always tried to arrange overnight stops there, but on one occasion, Admiral Wood was not happy with an overnight stop at Minneapolis. He and staff members checked in at the Nicolet Hotel and apparently had quite a party. They were late arriving for our departure the next day, which was unusual and the Admiral seemed not too pleasant. As it turned out, he had been "rolled," losing his wallet and everything in it.

Approaching Washington, DC, I was advised that we were number thirty-two in a stack and that there was an Army B-25 Mitchell bomber making an unauthorized approach to Washington National Airport. Everyone was alerted; any approaches would be made at their own risk. I held for a while and then advised approach control to either clear me down or clear me to my alternate. I was not concerned about the B-25 because he was on visual flight rules, somewhere in the vicinity of National Airport. We were landing at Anacostia. We made it down with no problems, although I never did hear what happened to the B-25.

I arranged for quarters at the air station for my crew, and then took my orders over to get them endorsed. I was met personally by the executive officer and was surprised to see that it was Cdr. Renfro; he had been executive officer at Sitka when I had temporary duty there. It was quitting time, so he drove me over to his quarters on the base and poured a few drinks.

He seemed to have something on his mind, and it finally came out. He asked me what I thought his chances would be if he tried

Bud Bodding's Lockheed R5O undergoing a 120-hour check.

Douglas R4D parked on the mat at Adak. August 1943. *U.S. NATIONAL ARCHIVES.*

for an appointment as Governor of Alaska. That was, of course, before statehood and the job was a political appointment. I answered, "I don't know how that type of politics functions, so I really can't answer your question." A while later he called the Navy Transportation Office and had them deliver me to the Statler Hotel where I stayed during my Washington sojourn.

Shortly after returning to Adak, Admiral Whiting received orders and was replaced as COM 17 by Admiral Ralph Wood. Soon after this I had a trip to Dutch Harbor, Kodiak, and Anchorage with four civilians aboard. Their names were Mike O'Riely, Jim Beary, and two others, Bob and John; I had no idea who they were. They spent a day at each stop, and then we returned to Adak.

A few days later, word came out that all flying east of Adak to Kodiak was cancelled. Rumor had it that President Roosevelt was arriving on a Navy cruiser. I had a call from Jim Beary saying he, Bob, and John wanted to go to Dutch Harbor. I advised him that all flights up the chain had been cancelled, but he asked me to call for my clearance anyway and said that it would be granted. Later, Jim told me that they were all Secret Service agents on the president's staff. Mike O'Riely, who was in charge, stayed in Adak to await the president's arrival. I believe that we were the only flight that day between Adak and Dutch Harbor.

Talking with Jim Beary en route, I learned that my crew and I had been thoroughly investigated before flying the group. They pretty much knew our life histories. We remained in Dutch Harbor until the president's cruiser approached the area, and then went on to Kodiak. The same procedure was followed there as well as the other stops.

Next we went on to Juneau. One afternoon, Jim, Bob, John, and I were in the lounge at the Elk's Club when someone looked in the lounge and then immediately turned away. Beary said, "Let's get out of here." We left immediately. The person in question was walking up the street and Jim asked if I knew him. I did, so back we went to our drinks. They were very thorough and suspicious.

While I was in Juneau, I stayed with my folks. They had no idea of the purpose of my trip. The president's cruiser arrived in the Juneau area, and we departed for the Annette Island Airport. I understand that Casey Moran, who was in the Coast Guard at the

Admiral Ralph Wood, third from left, arriving on Attu. April 24, 1945.
U.S. NATIONAL ARCHIVES.

time, boarded the cruiser in Juneau, took the president fishing in the Cape Fanshaw area.

Our next stop was NAS Sand Point in Seattle. We took a cab down to the area of the railroad station. We located the president's rail cars, which were well hidden on sidetracks. We went aboard, and I was introduced to a number of people and the president's dog, Fala. Jim, Bob, and John had quarters on the president's cars. We poured a couple of drinks, and then I took a cab to the New Washington Hotel where I had a room.

I was advised that I would be contacted soon regarding further orders, and a few days later I was told to be out at Pier 91 at 5:00 p.m. I took a cab out to the entrance gate where I was asked my name and to show identification. The guard made a short phone call, and a Navy shore patrol appeared and escorted me down to an area where the president's rail cars were now parked. I had noticed that no one else was being allowed in or out of the entrance gate.

The five o'clock shift was just getting over and nobody was allowed to depart. Jim Beary met me, and together we walked down to where Roosevelt's cruiser had just docked. They moved him in a wheelchair to one of his train cars. Beary followed him and returned shortly to escort me aboard the train.

The president was alone, and after being introduced Beary left. Roosevelt thanked me for my services and talked about catching salmon with guide Casey Moran. Jim Beary returned and escorted me to the gate. I noticed that the Pier 91 workers were still being held. I imagined they were not released until after the president's train left. I cannot imagine that they were very happy with President Roosevelt, or maybe they did not know what was going on. Jim told me he had hoped I would fly his group to Washington, DC, but they were traveling by train instead. I was free to return with my crew to Adak.

Soon after I returned to Adak, Admiral Wood asked me what kind of shape the Lodestar was in. After checking logbooks, it was decided that the aircraft was due for a major overhaul, so on September 24, 1944, I received orders to deliver Lockheed Lodestar, Bureau Number 12454 to Aircraft Industries, Glendale, California, for overhaul. The Admiral asked how long it would take and what I would be doing during that time. I figured it would be about a month and told him I would like to take an advanced instrument course while I was waiting for the work to be completed.

I delivered the aircraft as directed and my crew and I checked into the Glendale Hotel. I soon received orders to proceed to NAS Atlanta, Georgia, in time to report on October 12 for instrument training. I took a train from Los Angeles and arrived a day prior to my reporting date. I learned that Lt. Cdr. Hoyle, whom I previously mentioned as being stationed at Kodiak, was now executive officer at NAS Atlanta. On my first day there I was summoned to his for a friendly talk. Hoyle told me that there was an 11:00 p.m. curfew for student officers, but that it did not apply in my case and he wrote me a pass so I could come and go as I pleased.

I also met with Lt. Tom Case with whom I had served with in Sitka and Adak. He had just completed his instrument course and had orders to Roanoke, Virginia, for two weeks of transport training.

One day, returning from an instrument training flight, Lt. Cdr. Dawson, whom I had relieved as pilot on the Lodestar, met me. He had been assigned as executive officer at NAS Corpus Christi, Texas. They had a hurricane warning, and he had ferried a station aircraft for safekeeping. That night, Dawson, Hoyle and I did the town, and I had my first opportunity to use my "after 11 p.m. pass."

Actually the instrument course went pretty easily. We flew Twin Beech aircraft and were given a very comprehensive Link trainer, simulated cross-country course. I had become quite proficient in instrument flying, learning by doing, and I found I had much more actual instrument flying than my flight instructor. With still a week to go, my instructor told me I was wasting his and my time and to just take off and return a week later to pick up my diploma.

Prior to my departing Adak for Glendale, the Navy had come out with a new issue of instrument cards to qualified pilots. A pink card authorized little more than authority to fly on top of an overcast. A white card authorized instrument flight with concurrence of the operations officer at the departing station. A green card authorized the pilot to clear in any weather at his own discretion. I learned that only white cards were issued after completing the course at Atlanta, and I had already been issued a white card before departing Adak.

Tom Case had completed his course at Roanoke and showed up in Atlanta at the time I was told to take off. He was driving to his new duty station at Banana River, Florida. We had a mutual friend from Adak, Lt. Bob Vadnais, who was going through PB4Y-2 Privateer training at Jacksonville, so Case suggested that I join

The PB4Y Privateer was the Navy's highly modified version of the Army Air Force B-24 Liberator. *U.S. NATIONAL ARCHIVES.*

him, and we would visit Bob. We left Atlanta, drove all night, and arrived at Jacksonville the next day. Lt. Vadnais had completed his training and in a few days was driving to his new duty station in San Diego. We had a good visit, and they even talked me into playing a game of golf. I then took a train back to Atlanta. I received my certificate of completion of the instrument course, and a new white card.

Travel orders (three days plus travel time) were issued to me for Los Angeles. I boarded a train and proceeded to New Orleans, figuring that would be a good place to spend a couple of days. After checking into a hotel, I went down to the bar to have a drink.

There was only one other person sitting there. He looked up and said, "Can I buy you a drink, sailor?" He looked like a friendly person so I joined him. After awhile he said he was calling a cab and going down to the French Quarter and invited me along. We went to Arnauds Restaurant and Bar where the doorman addressed him. We walked through the restaurant and the kitchen and back to a very plush bar. There were a dozen or so people there, and they all seemed to know my friend. Everyone was very cordial, drinks flowed freely, and later an excellent dinner was enjoyed, all at no charge. On inquiry, I found that my new friend was a member of the family that owned Arnauds and that he was the black sheep of the family. Regardless, it was a fun night.

I spent another day in New Orleans and then boarded a train for Los Angeles and on to Glendale, arriving on Thanksgiving Day. I checked back in at the Glendale Hotel, and then contacted my crewmembers who were also staying there. They had been having a good time with no duties and no one to report to. They would occasionally go out to Aircraft Industries and check on our Lodestar's progress and they advised that things were going very slowly. The next morning I discovered that the Lodestar had been well torn down and nothing was being done toward completion; I was told that they were having trouble getting parts. I advised the Admiral of the progress, or lack of it, and I followed up with reports over the next couple of months. My crew and I would check on what was being done a couple times a week. In the meantime, the Silver Room, a bar located in the basement of the Glendale Hotel became our main hang out.

In the latter part of November, I found I was eligible for promotion from lieutenant (JG) to lieutenant. I had to take a physical examination so I took a bus to NAS San Pedro and had the physical done.

A week after I had returned to Glendale from Atlanta, Lt. Vadnais arrived, on his way to San Diego. I rode along with him to San Diego and then drove his car back to Glendale because he had no use for it the next week.

I went along on a training flight with him in the PB4Y-2. It was a long-distance training flight, about seven hours. It was cold and not very comfortable, but it did qualify me for the required four-hour flight time so I could get my flight pay for the month.

There were a number of Navy aircraft in overhaul at Aircraft

Industries, including Lockheed R5Os and Douglas R4Ds. One plane that seemed to be getting special attention was a Lockheed assigned to the Secretary of the Navy. When it was completed, my crew and I were asked to test hop it. We took it out, completed the air checks, and flew around for four hours, thereby qualifying us for our flight pay that month.

Apparently Admiral Wood got tired of waiting for the Lodestar to be overhauled. Accordingly, I received a dispatch dated January 26, 1945, directing me, my co-pilot LeRoy Hennrich CAP, Kenneth Wright ACMM, and Ray Scott ACRM to report by dispatch to ComFair (Commander Fleet Air) Seattle. They advised us that R5O BU# 99093 would be ready for flyaway Seattle on February 14. On February 3, I received a dispatch that R5O aircraft 99093 was no longer slated for COM 17. I would be advised of a replacement airplane when one became available. I found out later that the subject aircraft had been taken over from Pan Am and was an older plane. I am sure that the Admiral was not about to be saddled with an older aircraft, which was why he turned it down.

On February 19, 1945, I received the following message from ComFair Seattle, "Direct Lt. Bodding and crew report to originator as soon as possible in connection ferrying R4D, BU# 17222 x Plane now en route Seattle. Assigned to Info Adee."

The R4D was the military version of the Douglas DC-3 and neither my crew nor I had any experience on that type of aircraft. By noon the next day, my crew and I reported in at Seattle, but the aircraft had not yet arrived. It arrived late on February 22 and was turned over to me. The aircraft was not plush; it had twenty-one McAther seats (barely comfortable) and a large cargo door.

The Operations Officer at NAS Seattle had quite a bit of time in the R4D aircraft and agreed to give me some check time. The evening after the aircraft arrived, we took off at dusk and I got to make my first landing at Pasco, Washington. Then we flew on to Portland, Oregon, and finally back to NAS Seattle, arriving early in the morning. Everything went well, and my check pilot stated I would have no trouble with the aircraft.

On February 25 we departed for Adak in the R4D with a dozen or so Navy enlisted men on board headed for assignment. Annette

Lieutenant (JG) Bud Bodding. 1944.

Lt. Bud Bodding, the admiral's pilot, in sunglasses.
U.S. NATIONAL ARCHIVES.

Island was a fuel stop, and I made my first daytime landing in the R4D. We proceeded on to Anchorage and were verbally directed to remain there to await orders from Cdr. Horton who was also on staff COM 17. When he arrived, he presented me with written orders as follows, "Subject: Temporary Additional Duty: On receipt of these orders, you will report to Commander John A. Horton Jr. for such temporary additional duty as may be assigned you as pilot of flag plane R4D BU No.17222." Cdr. Horton advised me that Admiral Fletcher would arrive at Anchorage and we would fly him to Washington, DC. Lt. Cdr. Cote, a pilot assigned to Naval Air Transport VR5, also would accompany us. He was to check me out on the R4D and instruct me as he saw fit.

We departed Anchorage on March 4, 1945, and arrived Washington, DC two days later. Cote and I checked into the Statler Hotel. Admiral Fletcher remained in Washington, and on March 9 we departed for San Diego with Cdr. Horton aboard. At the Anacostia Airport, Cote and I talked to two Navy nurses who were

Lt. Bud Bodding, other aircrew, and R4D.

The Bodding R4D crew. 1945.

trying to hitch a ride to Greenville, South Carolina. We figured that would be a good fueling stop, so we took them aboard.

Cdr. Horton had no objection, but I think he was a bit annoyed when we invited them forward, where they remained for the entire trip. After departing Greenville we flew all night with further fuel stops at Dallas and El Paso, arriving in San Diego at noon on March 10.

The next day we arrived at Seattle for a two-day stop. We then went to Anchorage where Lt. Cdr. Cote left us. I enjoyed his company and appreciated what I had learned from him about the R4D. Finally we flew home to Adak where we arrived on March 15, 1945. That was ten days short of six months from the time I left to have the Lodestar overhauled.

At Adak we landed on the new Navy field at Andrew Lagoon, where we had been assigned a hangar. The day after we arrived, I was advised that the Admiral wanted to go to Attu. Bob Ellis was now commanding officer of NAS Attu and I was invited to stay at his quarters. The evening before our scheduled departure, Bob hosted a party for the Admiral. A brief phone call interrupted the party and everyone left at once — the C-3 hangar, where my airplane was located, was on fire! We drove down to a raging inferno, my airplane included. We never did get any details on the cause of the fire, except years later in a discussion with one of my ex-crew members who told me he thought that a jealous NAS Attu mechanic had torched the aircraft. The next day, Admiral Wood, his staff members, and my crew and I caught Naval Air Transport back to Adak.

"What now?" I wondered. About a week later I received orders for us to proceed to NAS Seattle via Naval aircraft. We were to take delivery of Naval Aircraft R4D Bureau Number 33819, which we recognized to be an aircraft that had been in overhaul in Glendale all the time we were waiting for the Lodestar to be overhauled.

Accompanying the plane was a chief aviation machinist who had been waiting all through the overhaul. We knew him quite well from our association in Glendale. He advised us that our Lodestar had been overhauled and departed, but to where he did not know. This time we were in Seattle for a couple of weeks getting additional radio gear, etc., installed.

Attu was commanded by Bob Ellis late in the war.
ELLIS FAMILY PHOTO.

Above: Hangar fire aftermath. L to R: Bud Bodding, Bob Ellis, Adm. Wood.
Below: Remains of Bud's R4D after the hangar fire on Attu. *U.S. Navy photographs.*

Bud, crew, and the admiral's R4D.

The admiral's pilot and R4D.

The aircraft was very plush with twelve seats and a separate compartment with a lounging area. We were pretty well set up with our hangar at the field, Andrew Lagoon, Adak. There was one problem though; the Admiral and staff were at Finger Bay, about a twelve-mile drive past the Army landing field. For convenience, anytime the Admiral wanted to fly, we would ferry the airplane over to the Army field for pickup. I also would have to drive over to Finger Bay quite often on business.

We were allotted an International pickup, which we kept quite busy. Frequently, the crew would be using it when I needed it. One day, while they were driving past the end of the Army field, my crew noticed an Army Jeep that had been driven off the road and into the bay. Somehow they got a rope on it and pulled it out. They towed it on to our hangar where they got it running. They also built an enclosure for it and painted it in Navy colors. From then on I had my own transportation. When we finally moved out of Adak, I left the Jeep parked by the hangar with the keys in it.

The Army and Navy boys were always trying to outdo each other. Once, my crew was over at the Army area and noticed a fenced-in lot with a large number of cases under a tarp. One of the guys climbed over the fence and passed over one of the cases. They threw it into the truck and drove on over to the Navy area. They opened the case, and were we ever surprised; it was full of canned spinach!

One day I received a call that a Naval Air Transport pilot was on Adak to give me an instrument check flight, the first one ever, except at Instrument Flight School at NAS Atlanta. I rode the check and apparently did okay, because on completion he presented me with a green card, which authorized me to clear on an instrument flight in any weather at my own discretion. As the war progressed, the Army Air Field at Adak was upgraded. Both runways were lengthened and blacktopped. When the Sea Bees built the Navy field, it was winter. Frozen mud was smoothed over and steel mat was laid. Summer came and the ground thawed. With it, the steel mat started sinking in spots, making takeoffs and landings like roller coaster rides. Attempts to repair the field were made, but it was essentially hopeless. Finally, the field was permanently closed. We continued to keep our Navy quarters, but moved the aircraft to the Army field.

We were in Attu when VJ Day was declared. We returned to Adak, and soon after COM 17 and staff moved to NAS Kodiak. Ground transportation was at a premium, but by then I pretty well knew my way around. I went to the motor pool and advised them that the Admiral wanted me to have a car. I knew they would not question it. They assigned me a very nice pre-war Plymouth coupe. The next problem was getting the ever tightly rationed gas for it. Captain W.F. Bull Dawson, whom I relieved as the Admiral's pilot, was now Commanding Officer of NAS Kodiak.

I went to him and said that I had been assigned a car but had no gas. He asked me if the car was for business or monkey business; I told him a little of both. He supplied me with a card authorizing unlimited gas and a windshield sticker allowing me to drive anywhere on Kodiak Island.

Peacetime had pretty well taken over, and there were now a number of civil service women employed at NAS Kodiak. Every Saturday night, there were formal dances at the Officer's Club. I don't know where they got them, but I never noticed any of the women wearing the same gowns twice.

On a monkey business trip returning from the town of Kodiak with another Lt., we stopped and picked up two lady hitchhikers. By the time we got to the base we had dates for the Saturday night dance. My date, Gladys Honeycut, was quite attractive and we started going steady.

We were soon made aware of the discharge point system, and I found I would be eligible for discharge on November 1, 1945. A while before, I had been assigned a new copilot, Lt. Max Roushman. It was my understanding that he was to take over as the Admiral's pilot when I left the service. On October 24, I was summoned to the Admiral's office.

On the occasion of the first ground controlled approach (CGA) to Attu. Summer 1945. Bud Bodding (back to camera); Adm. Fletcher, fourth from left; Adm. Brown, fifth from left.

Admiral Fletcher departs Attu. New hangar, replacing the one in which Bud's R4D perished, nearing completion. Summer 1945. *U.S. Navy photograph.*

Bud and copilot in the R4D. 1945.

Bud and fellow pilots unwinding at the Officer's Club, 1945.

He asked me if I would consider postponing my discharge date to January 15, 1946 because he was planning a trip to Washington, DC, followed by some leave in Palm Springs. The plan was to drop him off and then ferry the R4D to Seattle. Lt. Roushman, the rest of the crew, and I would then take thirty days leave after which we would meet the Admiral in Seattle. Also, he wanted Lt. Roushman to have more check time before taking over the aircraft. I was having a good time in Kodiak, and another trip to Washington, DC, sounded just fine. And thirty days leave over the holidays would not be bad either.

The Admiral made the request for my duty extension to the Chief of Naval Personnel and it was approved. Accordingly, we departed Kodiak on November 25, 1945. Overnight stops were made at Seattle, Bismarck, and Minneapolis, arriving in Washington, DC, on November 28.

I learned that one reason for the trip was so that Admiral Wood could attend the Army–Navy football game. I was invited to join the group but declined because I was not a football fan. As it turned out, Navy lost so the Admiral probably was not in a good mood. We departed Washington on December 6, overnighted at Dallas,

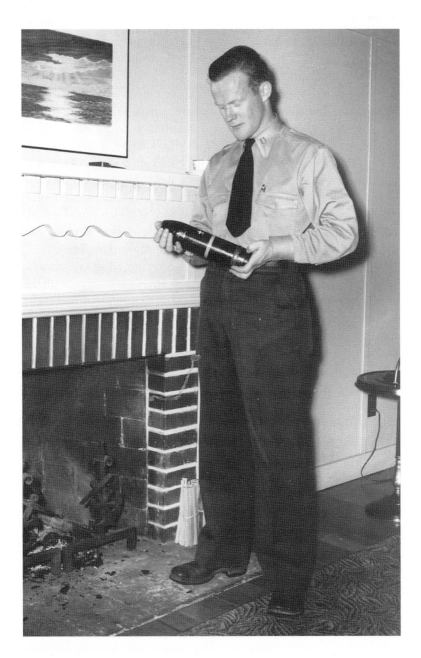

At home for Christmas in Juneau. 1945.

and then flew on to Palm Springs where we dropped the Admiral. The crew and I then overnighted at Burbank, arriving at NAS Seattle on December 8.

As ordered, I left the aircraft with Naval Air Transport VR5 in Seattle. On December 10, I started my leave. Pan Am in Alaska was then under Navy contract, so I caught them to Juneau to spend Christmas with my folks. Before leaving Kodiak, I told my lady friend, Gladys, it would be nice if she could get a week off and join me for Christmas. She came to Juneau and before she left I had an engagement ring on her finger.

My leave was over on January 8, 1946, at which time I reported back, picked up my airplane, and then flew on to Kodiak with the Admiral on board. That was my last flight. On January 23, 1946, I was released from active duty and returned to my job with Ellis Air Lines in Ketchikan. During my time in the Navy, with the exception of the thirty-day leave I took in December, I had taken no time off, so I still had two months and eighteen days leave on the books, making my actual release April 10, 1946, with pay to that date.

Gladys wanted to stay with her job at NAS Kodiak until September, at which time she planned to come to Ketchikan, and we would make plans for the future. But things had changed by the time she got to Ketchikan, and she decided to return to Kodiak. That was okay by me, and I got my ring back.

I remained in the Naval Reserve (inactive) until September 1, 1955, at which time I received notification of honorable discharge from the U.S. Naval Reserve. I had no desire to stay in the reserve because I had no interest in keeping up the required qualifications. In conclusion, I would say that I always went along with the statement, "Never volunteer for anything in the military."

All of my three and one-half years of military service was considered overseas duty for which I collected overseas pay. This was beside the fact that my duty was in Alaska *and* my residence was in Alaska. There was one possible exception; I do not recall if I received overseas pay for the time I spent in Glendale and Atlanta, but I think I did because my duty station was always listed in Alaska.

Interestingly, in retrospect, when I reported for duty as an ensign at Kodiak, apparently nobody, including myself, took the time to read and understand my orders. There were pages and pages of Navy lingo, and I know I could not decipher it. I was classed as Aviation Volunteer Probationary (AVP). The orders read that I was to take a prescribed course in Navy regulations, which I never did.

Included was a letter of authority to solo Naval aircraft, renewable annually. I was not to fly more than fifty miles from my base. The way I interpreted my orders, after my discharge, was that my primary job was to accompany and instruct pilots new to the Alaskan sector regarding local flying conditions. Had anyone read and digested my original orders, I am sure that my Navy career would have been much different.

As stated before, my first flight was to Cordova, well over the fifty-mile limitation. I often wondered why I was chosen as the Admiral's pilot for the Alaskan sector of the 13th Naval District and then the 17th Naval District. I assume that the glowing recommendation of Captain Tate of NAS Sitka on my application and my right decision while accompanying Admiral Reeves on the PBY flight to Seattle from Sitka had a lot to do with it. Also, my flying experience in Alaska certainly helped.

The Aleutian chain may not have been the most desirable place in the world for flying, but like everything else, it is all in what you are used to.

One thousand miles southwest of Anchorage, a Navy R4D flying over Islands of the Four Mountains. July 1943. *U.S. NATIONAL ARCHIVES.*

The Gareloi Volcano, 125 miles west of Adak, serves as a backdrop for this R4D. *U.S. NATIONAL ARCHIVES.*

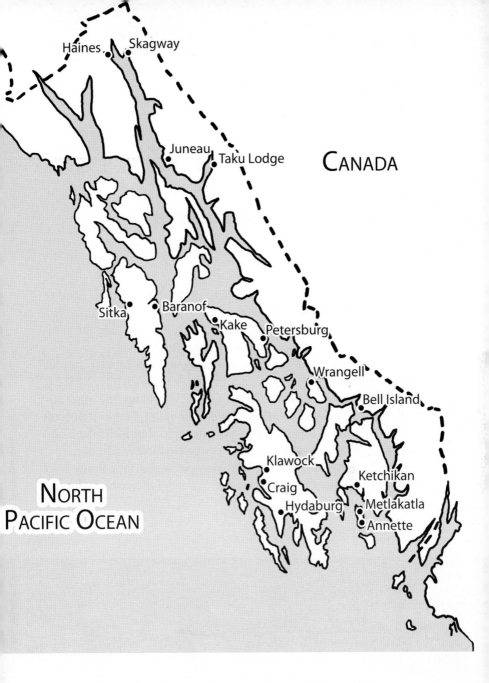

Haines • • Skagway

Juneau • • Taku Lodge

CANADA

Sitka • • Baranof
• Kake

Petersburg •

Wrangell •

Bell Island •

Klawock •
Craig • Ketchikan •
Hydaburg • • Metlakatla
• Annette

NORTH
PACIFIC OCEAN

PART THREE:
POST-WAR THROUGH RETIREMENT

VII: Growing the Airlines

After my discharge from active duty in the Navy, I proceeded to Ketchikan and to my job with Ellis Air Lines. Bob Ellis had returned sometime previously. He was busy reorganizing the company and getting it geared up for post-war operations.

The number one priority was the purchase of two surplus Grumman Goose amphibian aircraft. Bob had flown one, N88821, from Georgia to Ketchikan. At the time of my return, the other aircraft, N86590, was weather-bound with pilot Hugh Ramsdell somewhere in California. Eventually he arrived in Ketchikan, and the two aircraft were hangared for conversion to civilian use.

The number one Goose, 821, was converted to a flying boat and was to be used mainly on the Wrangell–Petersburg–Juneau

Ellis Air Lines operations in Ketchikan.

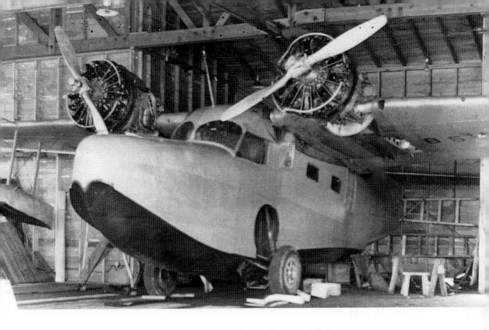

Ellis Air Lines first Goose, undergoing conversion from military to civil air transport configuration.

route. The other aircraft, 590, would be used on the Craig–Klawock–Hydaburg route and to the Annette Island Airport. By 1947 Pan Am started commercial service to Seattle and Juneau through the Annette Island Airport. Ketchikan passengers were handled by boat through Metlakatla.

Also returning from the military were former employees Rodger Elliott and Wes Sande. Both had been trained as pilots in the Army and had received their commercial pilot licenses. Norm Gerde, an Ellis accounting employee, had received his commercial license and was flying for Ellis during the latter war years.

As I recall, company aircraft at the time were two Bellancas, one Stinson, and a two-place Aeronca that had been purchased from Norm Gerde. Also, we soon added a third Grumman, N1019N, which was purchased from Tony Schwamm of Petersburg Air Service.

Sometime in the spring of 1947, Betty Hofstad, the young lady originally from Petersburg, whom I had met before the war, was visiting relatives in Ketchikan. We renewed acquaintance, and by

Ellis Air Lines main hangar facility on the Ketchikan waterfront.

View from within Ellis terminal. Ellis family photo.

Bud landing a Goose in Ketchikan.

the time she returned to Petersburg, we were engaged with a wedding date set for November 1, 1947.

Business was good at the airline. We had started flying Pan Am passengers between Annette and Ketchikan. Summer was on us, together with its long workdays. On one occasion, I was flying my last trip of the day with just one passenger from Annette to Ketchikan. The passenger occupied the copilot seat in the Grumman, and we were engaged in conversation enroute. I approached for a grease-on (exceptionally smooth) landing and, quite suddenly, we stopped. Water was all around us in the cockpit and we scrambled to get out through the rear cabin door. The funny thing was, my passenger beat me out. The airplane, by this time, was floating nose down. The company utility boat hurried out and plucked us off the wreck, which was then towed to the beach. We were wet, but unhurt.

We were taken to the hospital where we spent the night. Imagine my embarrassment though. I had forgotten to crank up my wheels for the water landing. The main damage to the aircraft was demolition of the entire nose section including the windshield.

One of the results of my accident, and further wheels-up land-

Chief Pilot Bud Bodding. *Ellis family photo.*

ings on fields by other pilots, was a horn that was incorporated together with the radio. When the radio transmitter was on airport tower frequency for wheel landings, the horn would blow when throttling back if the wheels were up. Likewise, when landing on the water when on company frequency, the horn would blow on approach if wheels were down.

Things were quite hectic as the airline grew. In my case, I was vice-president in charge of operations, member of the board of directors, chief dispatcher (keeping track of all of the flights and scheduling), chief pilot, pilot of aircraft, and solo check pilot. With long summer days, I felt I was trying to do too much. Accordingly, I turned the chief pilot and check pilot job over to Wes Sande.

There were many interesting flights, including one in particular, which to this day I do not know how I could have handled better. On that occasion, I had delivered a very attractive woman to Waterfall, apparently to visit Curly, the watchman. This was in a Bellanca aircraft, and the lady was wearing a beautiful fur coat. The Bellanca was nosed-in to the float, and it was necessary for her to walk forward and duck under the wing struts to disembark. In doing so, she lost her balance and overboard she went. Curly and I got her out, very wet and cold. She assured us that she was okay, and up the float they went.

A couple of days later on a trip to Craig and Waterfall, I had mail and one passenger for Waterfall. The passenger was a Coast Guard chief. En route, I noticed he was nipping from a pint whiskey bottle. I wondered why he was going to Waterfall. By the time we got to Craig, he was quite inebriated. I left him half asleep in his seat and went up to our office where I received a message from Coast Guard Ketchikan instructing me not to take my passenger to Waterfall under any circumstances. Putting two and two together, I concluded that the chief must be the husband of the lady I had previously taken to Waterfall. Deliberating on what to do, I returned to the plane where my passenger was well passed out, sitting crouched over with his head down. A pistol was loosely hanging out of his left trouser pocket. I reached over, pulled it out, and put it in the baggage compartment.

I figured that the police in Craig could not do much good, and in his condition with the bottle now empty, I could make Ketchikan and he would never know the difference, which is exactly what happened. Coast Guard MPs met the plane and had quite a time getting him out, although he was quite meek. I am sure that it would have been quite different had we proceeded to Waterfall. Yes, the gun was fully loaded.

The company boat was an important part of the lives of most Ellis employees. There were a number of fifty-foot Coast Guard utility boats anchored in a cove at Pennock Island. They were finally declared surplus and turned over to the War Assets Board for disposal. We agreed that it would be nice if the company could acquire one of the cruisers and, on checking, we found that the boats would first be offered to people with veteran's preference.

I had a flight to Juneau the day before the proposed sale, so I went up to the War Assets office to get further particulars. I found that I was eligible to bid using my veteran's preference and then could turn the boat over to the company. On the return flight to Ketchikan, the person I had talked to at the War Assets happened to be a passenger riding the copilot's seat. I had quite a talk with him en route and when we arrived at Ketchikan he said, "See you at the sale tomorrow."

The boats were listed at $2,300 to $2,500, and names were to be drawn. Mine was the second name. I will never know if my name was actually drawn or if the War Assets person just wanted me to have the boat. There were over sixty people trying to get one of the boats.

Bob Ellis and I had inspected the boats, and we got the one that was number one on our list with a cost of $2,500. We named the boat *ZOOMIE,* which is what naval aviators were referred to. I turned the boat over to the airline for the same $2,500 I paid for it.

Throughout the years, the *ZOOMIE* played an important part in the lives of our employees. It was available to any employee after a proper checkout, and the cost to them was a little more than the price of gas. A reservation book was kept, so those wishing to use the boat signed up for their days. The most preferred destination was Bell Island Resort and its swimming pool. In the autumn, Rocky Pass near Kake for deer and duck hunting was number one on the list.

Zoomie, the Ellis Air Lines company boat.

The procedure was to form a number of parties, each with a Grumman pilot. The first group would take the boat to the hunting area. Subsequent trips were flown in and the pilot on board the *ZOOMIE* would then ferry his hunting partners, gear, and game to Ketchikan. Arrangements for aircraft were similar to the *ZOOMIE*. For a little more than the cost of gas and a pilot available, employees could utilize the aircraft for recreational purposes.

The *ZOOMIE* led a long and charmed life, never having any serious accidents, just a few minor groundings. The boat was well maintained, with Mel Wick and his ground maintenance crews spending numerous hours keeping it in shape. With the Coastal–Ellis merger there was no longer personnel available on company time, and interest in use declined. After the merger with Alaska Airlines in 1968, since one half of the merger had a perks boat but the other half did not, in order to eliminate any source of malcontent I made an offer to buy the *ZOOMIE* for just what I sold it to Ellis: $2,500. The offer was accepted.

Prior to this, I had purchased a diesel-powered, thirty-eight-foot, ex-Coast Guard cruiser that I named the *SHEILA B* after my

Sheila Bodding and friend on the *Sheila B.*

daughter. The boat needed some care, and Paul Mattle allowed me to use his boathouse at Knudson's Cove to do the work. After spending the summer working on the boat, we made a few short cruises.

My mooring spot was at the Yacht Club Float. The boat was tied nose into the float and stern into Ketchikan Creek. The floats along the creek had been removed for maintenance. A very rainy October day caused Ketchikan Creek to go on a rampage. The result was that the *SHEILA B's* bow was pushed up on the float resulting in the stern submerging, leaving just a small part of the bow out of the water.

Fortunately my brother-in-law, Albert Hofstad, with the boat *Tonka* and another Petersburg seine boat were in town. With their help, we re-floated my boat. I had the engine cleaned up and running shortly. Back to Mattle's boathouse for another overhaul it went. I kept the *SHEILA B* for a while, but then on one fine spring day while walking down the float it became obvious to me that the *SHEILA B* would require a major paint job, so I took a loss and sold it.

Back to the *ZOOMIE,* after again becoming an owner, I took

Bud, at the Ellis dock, about to attach the hoist for lifting the
Goose to the main hangar.

in five other airline associates as partners, and we proceeded to get
the boat back in shape. It was no small chore, but was finally completed. The boat was put to good use, but my retirement was coming up. I sold my interest in anticipation of purchasing a new boat
and going into the charter business.

Numerous changes in our aircraft fleet were happening. We
kept adding Grummans. Eventually Ellis Air Lines had a fleet of
nine Goose aircraft. We sold the Aeronca that we had purchased
from Norm Gerde along with the Stinson aircraft. We then purchased two three-passenger Aeronca Sedans, which proved less
than satisfactory because they were somewhat underpowered.

Cessna had started building the 180, and they did look good.

Unfortunately, they did not work out either. With our first 180, I took an early morning charter flight to Juneau, returning to Ketchikan before 8:00 a.m. While walking up the ramp I looked down on the aircraft. The nose seemed to have a droop. I discovered that the two top motor mount supports were broken and spread apart. The only thing holding the engine on was the lower support. On further investigation, we found some Canadian operators had the same trouble with the early 180s.

Ellis Air had a total of three Cessna 180s. One was totaled when it ended up in the trees while circling a burning aircraft in the Telegraph Creek, British Columbia area; fortunately there were no injuries. The second Cessna, with company employees aboard, crash-landed after takeoff from Wilson Lake. There was one survivor, but the accident's cause was never determined. The third Cessna crashed on a mountain near Helm Bay. There were no survivors. The probable cause was carbon monoxide poisoning to the pilot. We decided that 180s were not for us and then went out of the single-engine aircraft business.

Earlier, we had grounded Bellanca NC256N and dismantled it. Our old favorite, Bellanca N11642 was returned to Bellanca Aircraft that was going to modernize it by installing flaps, a big cargo door, and other improvements. The factory sent a pilot to Ketchikan to ferry it to the east coast. The flight came to an abrupt stop a couple of hundred miles from its destination. On takeoff from a lake, the aircraft was demolished when the pilot failed to clear some electrical wires. Fortunately, there were no injuries.

November 1, 1947, was rapidly approaching. Betty Hofstad and her mother, Dorothy, arrived in Ketchikan and plans for our wedding went into high gear. Numerous invitations were sent and arrangements were made for the use of the Lutheran Church and Pastor Halvorsen. I took advantage of the idea that the bride's family would take care of all the pre-planning. When the wedding day arrived, things got more hectic. Bob Ellis had more or less passed the word that close friends and relations could fly free on company planes to Ketchikan for the occasion. All planes were kept busy on the west coast and Juneau routes. The church was filled to capacity and a large reception was held in the church facilities.

The next day, Betty and I departed via Pan Am on a trip to Seattle. We then picked up a company-owned Chrysler and made a trip as far as Arizona. On return to Ketchikan we occupied my place in the Revilla Apartments. The unit was small with a pull-down bed in the living room. We went house hunting and rather liked a home that was for sale on Bawden Street.

It was a small, two-bedroom house, with a one-bedroom apartment on the lower level. The price was $8,500. We were considering the purchase when one evening I received a phone call from the owner stating that if he could get out on the Alaska Steamship boat leaving at 9:00 p.m., he would reduce the price by $500. I called a friendly banker at his home. He advised that he would meet me at the bank at 6:30 p.m. By 7:30 financing was completed. The owner had his money and made his sailing deadline. The house was in a nice neighborhood, but had no garage. We had a fair view down the channel until a large apartment building was constructed, completely blocking our view.

Son Jim was born August 8, 1948, and occupied the spare bedroom. Son Eric was born July 17, 1950, and moved into the small bedroom with Jim. Betty and I decided that the house was a bit

Wedding day, November 1, 1947.   Cutting the wedding cake with bride, Betty.

small. I wanted a garage, and we both wanted a view. We liked the Second Avenue area and specifically a nice, white house at 2111 Second Avenue. I contacted a banker friend and advised him that if the house ever came up for sale, I was interested.

Shortly thereafter, I received a call to say that the house was on the market. I jumped into my car, drove downtown, and spotted the owner coming out of the post office. I cornered him and asked him about the house.

He was surprised that I knew about the proposed sale but gave me a price, saying that I was number two on the list. I received a call that evening stating that I was now number one. The next day Betty, the boys, and I went to look at the house, made a deal with the owner and bank, and then we moved in two weeks later. That was in January 1952. We rented out the Bawden St. house for a while and then sold it.

The Second Avenue house was new and not completely finished. Floors in the bedrooms and hallways were bare. The living room, however, had beautiful, hardwood floors. We soon found out that with the two boys running in and out, they were not practical. After re-finishing the floor once, we went to carpet.

Bud and Betty take delivery of a new Mercury in 1953.

Daughter Sheila was born December 31, 1956, making her a last minute income-tax deduction. With three children in the family, things were tight as far as sleeping space. I solved this by building a room for Jim in the basement, followed later by a room for Eric.

Son Jim, at the age of twelve, was quite interested in chemistry. After some research, he obtained some "ingredients" from a local drug store. He then tamped the mixture in a half-inch copper tube and lit it. At first it put out a thick, colored smoke. Carrying it to the back door, he said, "Mom, come and look!" Pressure had built up in the tube, which then blew up, taking off the four fingers on his right hand. Fortunately, a young lad with Boy Scout knowledge of first aid was walking by and put a tourniquet on Jim's arm. At the time, I was at Annette airport awaiting passengers and was told to return to Ketchikan immediately. Jim took his loss very well and had no trouble adjusting.

Betty and I were blessed with three wonderful children, mostly through Betty's efforts. Day after day and night after night while I was working and attending various meetings, etc., Betty was the one to see that the kids were raised properly.

There were, however, a few incidents during the kids' growing up years, especially for the boys. One night while I was at a meeting, Jim came home wet and muddy with some branches hanging from his clothes. He said he had been beaten up. In my absence Betty called my friend Dick Borch of the Ketchikan Rescue Squad. Dick came by, took one look at Jim and said, "Nothing wrong with him, he's just drunk."

Eric and one of his friends got in trouble at least once with the police. On one occasion a person sent a couple cars to Ketchikan in my care, intending to start a car rental service. Eric and a friend came by Ellis where the cars were parked. Eric said, "Dad can I drive the Volks, please?" I reluctantly answered, "All right, but stay in town." I then took a late flight to the west coast.

On my return, I discovered the car was missing. When I arrived home Eric was there, and I learned that the Volks was upside down in a ditch on the Ward Lake Road. Apparently, Eric had been giving his friend a driving lesson. The tow and repair bill came to $600. Eric and his friend were supposed to pay fifty dollars each per month. Eric paid his share, but the other boy didn't completely repay his.

As a young girl, Sheila always said she wanted to be a nurse and a mother. She never got to be a nurse, but I ended up with some nice grandkids.

Vacations at the airlines were taken during the slack periods from autumn through spring. One key priority was my ten-day hunting trip in October/November, and each year, Betty and I would also take a trip somewhere. We finally discovered Honolulu, courtesy of Pan Am. The kids were no problem. We could leave them with either my folks or Betty's.

On one occasion, my folks were staying on a farm in the Mt. Vernon area. They kept the two boys there during our ten-day visit to Honolulu. Driving up to the farmhouse on our return, I spotted the boys well dressed for the weather, playing in a mud puddle. Right then and there, Betty and I agreed it was time the kids started to enjoy the sunny vacations with us.

On summer days numerous beach parties were organized by Ellis employee wives, the pilots, and mechanics while other employees would join them when the day's work was done.

Bodding family Hawaiian vacation.

The Ellis bunch was a close-knit crowd and a number of us resided in the Second Avenue area. We could always find an excuse for a party at various homes. Also, the Elks Club on Main Street was a popular meeting place, usually on Saturday night where we would meet, party, dine, and dance.

The Civil Aeronautics Board (CAB) subsidized our airline operation quite heavily. Supposedly, they guaranteed us a profit of 6 percent on our investment. In turn we carried the first class mail and made it our number-one priority. Passengers came next. Our service was quite flexible, and we always tried to handle all passengers in our operating area on the day they wished to travel. In addition to our regular scheduled stops, we would pick up and drop off at other feasible stops in our area. To do this, we would operate many extra sections, plus divert the regular flights.

Mainline service from Seattle to Annette Island and then on to Juneau increased dramatically when Pacific Northern Airlines joined Pan Am. Both airlines wanted to serve the prime times, and they would arrive at Annette about twenty minutes apart, northbound and southbound. That would keep us busy, mostly with one-way hauls. We kept increasing our Grumman fleet and were looking at the possibility of larger aircraft. Alaska Coastal Airlines, our friendly competitor in Juneau, had added a Consolidated PBY Catalina to its fleet.

I had flown the Catalina during my Navy days and was not convinced that it was the answer to our Annette route. My contention was that we could handle passengers on a short haul of twenty-one miles better with two Grummans than with one Catalina, considering paper work, loading and unloading, plus time en route.

Our directors called a meeting, considered the purchase of a Catalina, and then voted against it. The very next day, another meeting was called and a tie vote came up. The missing director was contacted, and he voted in favor of the Catalina. Throughout the years, I never changed my mind. We had to acquire more float space, convert a building into a hangar, and build an elevator for the plane. On numerous occasions, the Catalina would taxi out for takeoff only to return to the float a few minutes later for mainte-

Bud on top of the Goose with a fishing party.

Many PBY Catalinas survived the war to fly again in airline service. Ellis family photo.

Coastal Ellis Air Lines' PBY Super Catalina at the Petersburg pull-out.

nance after problems surfaced during the magneto check on engine run-up. Then we would have to fly the Grummans instead.

After the merger with Alaska Coastal and then Alaska Airlines, I was, on one occasion, talking with my boss in Seattle. This was on a day when the Catalina was having magneto trouble. I said, "Pete, why don't we get rid of the Catalina?" He said, "What? I was always told we needed a Catalina in Ketchikan." I told him that he had not talked to me. The very next day, that Catalina was on its way south to Moses Lake, Washington, where it was sold.

As to medical emergency trips, our aircraft had rather narrow doors, and it was quite a chore to get a stretcher patient aboard. We eventually had very narrow stretchers built specifically to easily negotiate the doors. When I first started flying the Goose, though, I remembered a very heavy lady named Hattie Bagley Boyce who resided in Craig. It was my secret dread that someday she would be a stretcher case. My luck held out; she never became a medical emergency.

People in out-of-the-way places are prone to panic when emergencies do arise. Actually, there were very few that were serious

Coastal Ellis Goose in glacier takeoff.

during my flying days. One urgent call was from a logging camp on Etolin Island where a logger was seriously injured. Although no time was wasted, the person had died by the time I arrived.

One day the weather was so bad that we would not fly. A call came from Klawock where a man had fallen off a bridge and was pierced in the stomach by a lance-like tree branch, which could not be removed. I cranked up the Waco and had a touchy trip to Klawock in very marginal weather. The patient was in great pain and was very difficult to load in the plane. Departing Klawock, I observed a snow squall moving in the pass ahead. Darkness would soon arrive and there was no time to check other passes. I continued down Harris Creek Pass, running into snow very quickly. By rolling down the window for better vision, I could barely follow the river to salt water. But my passenger's time was not up and neither was mine. We arrived safely in Ketchikan and the patient was rushed to the hospital.

Another emergency occurred some time later at Neets Bay Logging Camp where a logger had been hit in the stomach by a large branch, which opened his abdomen and exposed his intestines, creating a very bloody, dirty mess. I wasted no time trans-

Grumman Goose tied up at Hydaburg.

porting him to Ketchikan, where a doctor and ambulance met us. Fortunately, the patient recovered in a few weeks. For a while I would see him walking around in a bent-over position. I do not know if drawing a bit of extra power on the Grumman's engines contributed, but on the next trip, I blew a cylinder.

Shortly after midnight one summer day, I received a call from Hydaburg that a young lady was in labor and needed medical attention. Rather than sending out another pilot, I decided to take the trip myself. I called one of our head mechanics, Ken Vanderwheele, and together we launched a Grumman, gassed it, and warmed it up while taxiing across the bay where I would not wake so many people on takeoff. It was a nice morning, and I landed at Hydaburg just at daylight while Ken manned the radio at Ketchikan. The pregnant girl and her mother arrived at the plane. After being airborne for a short time, the girl's mother came forward and advised, "The baby is coming."

There was nothing else I could do except add a bit more power and advise Ken to call a doctor and ambulance. Everything worked out. At the office while filling out my paperwork, I thought that the trip would make a great news story, but before the ambulance departed, the girl's mother came in. "Bud," she said, "don't tell the newspapers about this, because we don't know who the father is." So much for the news story. As for actual emergency flights, they were few and far between.

Throughout the early years of flying in Southeast Alaska, Ellis Air Lines of Ketchikan and Alaska Coastal Airlines of Juneau became the two predominating carriers. Alaska Coastal took care of the northern portion and Ellis took care of the southern part. For a number of years, the two companies were friendly competitors on the Ketchikan to Juneau scheduled route, including Wrangell and Petersburg. We shared terminals at Juneau and Ketchikan. The Wrangell office, personnel, and facilities were operated by Ellis. Likewise, the Petersburg station was operated by Alaska Coastal. The operation worked successfully for years. It was obvious that a merger would result in better scheduling, better service, and cost savings.

Accordingly, in 1962 the two companies became Alaska Coastal–Ellis Airlines. Later, for brevity, the name was shortened to Alaska Coastal Airlines. Headquarters were in Juneau. I elected to remain in Ketchikan with a new title of vice president, southern division. I was also a member of the board of directors of the new company. My workload remained the same. An agreement with the pilot's union allowed me to fly not more than sixty hours per month.

At the time of the merger, Bob Ellis retired. I was allowed to run the southern division pretty much as I wished. With the building of airports at Wrangell, Petersburg, and Sitka, it was obvious that we would have to concentrate on wheeled aircraft operation. Accordingly, service was started to Juneau, Petersburg, Wrangell, and Annette Island. The problem at the Ketchikan end was the twenty-one-mile shuttle, Annette to Ketchikan. Passengers from Wrangell/Petersburg traveling to the Lower 48 did benefit, however. Flights via Grumman aircraft to Wrangell, Petersburg, and Juneau were still available. Sitka–Ketchikan flights were handled by PBY Catalina aircraft.

As time progressed, it was obvious that Alaska Coastal, in order to grow, had to consider a Seattle route. Sitka was building an airport, and Alaska Airlines was considering a stop on its Seattle–Anchorage route. At the time Alaska Airlines was strug-

Downtown Ketchikan, circa 1960.

gling to make ends meet. A merger with Alaska Coastal would open the door for them to serve Southeastern Alaska out of Seattle.

After merger talks with Alaska Airlines and also Wien Airlines, it was decided to accept Alaska's offer. Accordingly, in 1968, Alaska Coastal Airlines ceased to exist.

As for my position, part of the agreement called for me to continue as a company officer. My new title was vice president, Ketchikan region. My duties remained pretty much the same. My job description was rather terse: perform the duties of Vice President. I was now limited to forty flying hours per month. With a bid procedure on flight trips, it was difficult to fly any of the preferred trips and still keep up with my other duties. Accordingly I resigned my VP position and went back to active flying.

The pilot's union advised me that I could become a union member by paying a number of years back dues. The alternative would be to pay monthly dues with no voice or vote in the union. I accepted the latter because I was never much of a union supporter. The company went along with the change and paid me a few extra bucks to keep them in touch with the Ketchikan operation. I was also assigned as the only Ketchikan-based Grumman check pilot. When I was due for a check, an FAA inspector was sent up from Seattle, which was a farce since none of them had any Goose time.

On completion of the Ketchikan Airport on Gravina Island, Alaska Airlines' need for Grummans would end. Plans were to turn local flights over to a substitute carrier. For some time I had said, "When the Goose goes, so do I." On August 24, 1972, I would be age fifty-five. Accordingly, I wrote the company indicating my plans to retire, effective with my last workday, October 31, 1972.

With the merger of Alaska Coastal, Alaska Airlines had authority to serve Southeast Alaska on the Seattle–Anchorage route. That was before deregulation, and airline routes were assigned and governed by the Civil Aeronautics Board. Western Airlines was serving Ketchikan through Annette Island. Alaska Airlines moved in and began serving Cordova, Yakutat, Juneau, Sitka, Petersburg, Wrangell, and Ketchikan on the Seattle–Anchorage route. The C.A.B. decided that the southeast area could not support both Western and Alaska Airlines. After hearings, it was decided that

Bud at the controls of a Goose.

Bud with Shell Simmons upon reaching 30 years of airline flying.

Alaska offered the better package. Accordingly, Western Airlines was booted out.

With the award of Southeast Alaska as an exclusive, Alaska Airlines started to prosper, although it was broke at the time. I have always maintained that being awarded an exclusive operation in Southeast Alaska was the only thing that saved Alaska Airlines from bankruptcy. Alaska has done an excellent job of serving the southeast. Where else do you see small towns like Wrangell and Petersburg served by a major carrier? Only in Alaska, by Alaska.

VIII: The Golden Years

I had made it a practice to attend the annual boat show in Seattle generally looking for an ideal boat to buy upon my retirement from the airlines. In 1968, Tollycraft came out with a thirty-eight-foot cruiser, which came close to my desire. In 1972, they built a forty-foot model, which was much closer to what I wanted. In January 1972, I attended the boat show as usual, although Betty did not accompany me. Before I left Ketchikan, she stated, "Don't buy a boat without me." On the second day of the boat show I called home saying, "Guess what?" Betty answered, "You bought a boat." She did not seem surprised or mad. She knew what I was up to. The boat, yet to be built, with a June 1 delivery was well-equipped: twin Caterpillar engines, Onan light plant, electric heat, electric stove, six bunks, two heads, and a pullout couch for sleeping in the pilothouse.

As retirement was coming close, the company essentially advised me to take off as I wished. The boat was built in Kelso, Washington, and trucked to Lake Union in Seattle. It arrived shortly after June 1. Betty and I would go down quite often to view finishing touches, including radar, radios, and the anchor winch. We departed Seattle on our new boat, the *MY TIME* on June 28, 1972, with a full crew. We

Bud's cruiser, *MY TIME* at Bell Island. June 1978.

overnighted at LaConner and then cruised on to Campbell River, British Columbia. Departing early the next day, we were just about thirty minutes out and had clutch problems with the left engine.

We returned to the float and found a burnt-out clutch due to an oil leak. The warranty covered the problem and replacement parts were installed, but apparently the problem was not cured. About an hour out of Campbell River, after the engine had time to warm up, I noticed an oil leak around an oil line fitting. We pulled into Kelsey Bay and called the Caterpillar people in Campbell River. They drove up and gooped up the fitting. A permanent repair was made after arrival in Ketchikan. Summer was coming to an end, and on days off we made a number of trips on the *MY TIME*.

My retirement was coming up in late October. I made my next-to-last flight to Wrangell on October 30, 1972, when I was afforded a great send off. I reserved my last flight on October 31 for Klawock, Craig, and Hydaburg. I felt I owed my job to the west coast people because that was Ellis Air Transport's main run when I was first hired.

Bud returns to Ketchikan on his retirement day.

I had a great send off at each town and was given one Tlingit and one Haida name: *Skowa* and *Snook*. I never found out what they meant, but I was assured that they were good names. I had threatened to drag my wheels on the Ketchikan Airport, which was under construction at the time. I had one pay passenger aboard and settled instead for a low pass over the tunnel and down Front Street a bit low.

On docking, I was greeted by family members, friends, fellow pilots, and other employees. Son Jim and wife Betty removed my pilot's cap and jacket, replacing them with my yachting cap and jacket, a fitting and pleasant end to my flying career. It was time for a change of clothes, a short interview at the radio station, and then a very large retirement party at the Elks Club.

Capt. Bodding after his last flight as an airline pilot.

Congratulations from fellow Alaska Airlines pilots upon Bud's retirement.

"The Old Man and the Sea." Captain Bodding, master of the *MY TIME.*

In the spring of 1973, retirement was put on hold since I was about to start my second career. The cruiser *MY TIME* was ready to go, and I accepted my first charter. A couple of timber cruisers had a job to do in the Mt. Jumbo area at Helta Inlet. It was March with weather still a bit unstable. We had to go around Cape Chacon, which can be a bit nasty. We lucked out, however, and had a fair trip. On the return, Chacon was okay. We had a following sea and a pretty good roll when crossing south Clarence Straits. I heard an unusual "ping" from the engine room, but thought little of it and proceeded to Ketchikan.

The next day I started the starboard engine and heard a distinct cylinder "blow" sound. A mechanic found a small metal particle that must have been left in the engine when it was assembled. The heavy roll in Clarence Straits apparently dislodged the particle, which passed through and bent an exhaust valve.

That was the last engine problem except for a few minor fuel problems. When I purchased the *MY TIME,* my plan was to keep it for ten years and then retire completely. I kept it for eleven. The *MY TIME* years were a lot of fun, and I met a lot of interesting people.

From airlines captain to boat captain. Bud with the *MY TIME*.

For a number of years, I had charters with the U.S. Geological Survey, which had its own rubber boat for working the shore areas and collecting rocks. Usually there were four people in their parties. They would leave the *MY TIME* early in the day and return late. They would take care of their own meals with only occasional help from me. The Geological Survey charters were from six weeks to two months. I had many other trips, some for cruising and fishing, while others were strictly for fishing. I was not interested in trips less than four days, and there was still time for trips with family and friends. We were frequent visitors at Yes Bay and Bell Island. Then too, there were our annual trips to Rocky Pass for deer and duck hunting. Betty and I also made a trip to Siberia, compliments of Alaska Airlines.

I traveled to, or over, practically all areas of interest to me, including all of Alaska and a large part of the Lower 48. Looking back through my life, there is nothing that I would change. There were a few ups and downs, but that just made it all the more interesting.

Epilogue

Dad's autobiography essentially winds down in the late 1980s. He started writing his memoirs as a result of Eric's strong suggestion that he do so. One evening, Dad became uncharacteristically expansive and started talking about the old days. Eric, who was up from Seattle for a brief visit said, "Dad, if you don't put all of this down on paper, there's no way we'll remember it all."

By that point, the three of us had left home and moved to Washington State. Jim, with his fifty-eight-foot steel long liner, became a commercial fisherman, crabbing off the Washington coast and fishing Alaskan waters for black cod and halibut. Eric went into Seattle's construction industry as a crane operator. Sheila was a stay-at-home mom and homemaker for her children and grandchildren until later in life starting work in retail.

Mom died on January 24, 1999, nearly seven years after having been diagnosed with Alzheimer's disease. We had suspected it earlier when she became much more forgetful. Mom and Dad still traveled down to Washington to see us at first, but then Dad, like a saint, took care of her by himself at home as the disease progressed. She remained in good spirits, but eventually spent many of her last days asleep. Dad was very patient with Mom as the Alzheimer's claimed her, and he treated her with kindness, love, and respect right up to the end. Only in the last few months did Dad enlist limited outside help, choosing not to put her into a nursing care facility. Mom's ashes were dropped from Jim's boat, *Aleutian Isle,* into the waters off Wrangell Narrows near Scow Bay, close to the community and home where she had grown up.

Mom and Dad Bodding reveled in their role as grandparents. Although Sheila and her children moved to Port Townsend, Washington in 1984, Greg and Mandy started growing up in Ketchikan, where Mom and Dad came close to spoiling them. There were special treats at the candy store and early driving lessons. Jim's daughter, Chelsea, has the fondest memories of her visits with Grandpa Bud since they each had a "sweet tooth." Chelsea had easy access to the special, sweets drawer in the kitchen cupboard.

Sheila's husband, Murray Hayes, is a commercial fisherman like his brother-in-law Jim, and was away from home for extended periods. When Sheila's daughter Tracy was born in September 1986, at the height of the fishing season, Mom and Dad came down to help out, and they were there again three years later when son Eddie was born. The free airline passes certainly facilitated the many trips from Ketchikan to Port Townsend for birthdays, graduations, ballet recitals, and football games. And then, the great-grandchildren started to arrive, adding even more dimension to Mom and Dad's happiness. Mandy gave birth to Jamieson on July 20, 1994, and on September 4, 1995, Greg's wife Cori had Jacob, followed by Mandy having Hailey on November 17, 1997.

Once we kids were out of the house, Mom started working for Alaska Ferries. She enjoyed those days and was terrific with the passengers, especially considering her knowledge of the area and the fact that she was a wonderful storyteller. Earlier, Mom and Dad both would go fishing with our Uncle Albert Hofstad who seined for herring and salmon on his boat, *Tonka*. After retiring from Alaska Ferries, Mom occasionally crewed on her brother's boat. Both Mom and Dad enjoyed long line fishing as sport with only a minimum of gear.

After retiring from his flying career, Dad contracted to have a forty-foot Tollycraft boat built. With the arrival in Ketchikan of his new charter yacht, *MY TIME*, Dad started his second career as a charter boat captain, getting into that business at just the right time. The Alaska marine ferry system was used not only by Alaskans in the 1970s, but had gained in popularity among tourists as a wonderful way to see Alaska. This brought many sportsmen to Ketchikan. It was not long before the big cruise ships started calling at Ketchikan. Dad accepted these changes, but his heart was probably back in the days when the canneries and loggers were the backbone of the Ketchikan economy. Still, he had a very good fishing business as the result of growing tourism, and even had a United States senator and astronaut or two as fishing clients.

Mom and Dad enjoyed traveling, especially to Hawaii and California, while we kids were young, and continued traveling after we all left, particularly to visit relatives in Washington. In the intermediate years, we enjoyed Hawaiian vacations with them. Mom in particular enjoyed the sand, surf, and warm breezes; Dad was usually content to nurse a cold beer in the shade of a banyan tree.

He was a very social man, but not oriented to municipal politics, although Mom did volunteer work to register voters. Dad was a founding member and former Commodore of the Ketchikan Yacht Club, and active in and a leader of fraternal and patriotic organizations such as Moose, Elks, and the American Legion. One reason he enjoyed being a Moose so much was the fact that its hall was right on the water, close to the old Ellis hangar. Yet, when he became a senior citizen, he was more than content to let younger men assume leadership of those organizations. Those groups and Ketchikan at large always thought highly of Dad, especially on such occasions as his being named Grand Marshall of the Fourth of July parade.

Some of Dad's projects had their lighter sides. He liked to grow potatoes in a level part of his front yard. It got to the point that the occasional tour bus operator would stop briefly in the street and point out the "famous Alaskan bush pilot" at work in his potato patch. When Dad was in his early 80s, one of his neighbors became so alarmed at Dad's getting up on the roof to work on his gutters that she came over and pleaded with Dad to get down. Dad simply said, "Why? I spent a lot of years much higher than this!" referring to his many hours of flying time.

When we were very young, we probably never really appreciated what a unique man Dad was, and what a remarkable career he had. We just took it for granted that he went off to work in the morning and came home at the end of the day like all of our friends' dads. For Eric, that changed on Career Day at school when Chief Pilot Captain G.A. Bodding talked about airline flying to a standing-room-only crowd of students. Eric subsequently heard more than one friend say, "Boy, your dad sure is cool."

We also benefited tremendously from the liberal policy Ellis Air Lines had regarding personal use of company planes. We occasionally got to fly with Dad on regular trips and frequently flew with him for fishing on remote, mountain lakes. The key word is "remote" since we would fly far into the interior, find fabulous trout fishing on pristine lakes, and cook our catch on the shore. We took it for granted, not knowing how lucky we were. Then there were flights up to Scow Bay where we landed on the water, headed for the shore, lowered the gear, and taxied directly onto the beach right in front of our grandparents' house. We all spent a lot of spare time down at the Ellis base in Ketchikan, much as Dad had done many years before at the seaplane base in Juneau.

With Jim, Dad could be a real prospector: for coral (a very specialized market), for natural spring water, and even searching for uranium by plane at low altitude with a Geiger counter.

Not all of our adventures were light and enjoyable. There was the day when a strong southeaster prohibited flying, but son Jim was reported missing out in his little fishing dinghy. Dad and Eric cranked up a Goose, barely got airborne in the gale, went out to search, and found the dinghy, drifting and apparently empty. Brokenhearted, they landed and were lucky to intercept the little boat in the howling wind. Jim was found, however, safe and sound underneath canvas casually trying to ride out the storm. Jim assured them that he was fine and absolutely refused to get into the plane; he was afraid his boat would break up on the rocky shoreline if he abandoned it. They had no choice but to leave him. Fortunately, everyone made it back to Ketchikan with no further problems.

One of Dad's consuming interests in his later years was the Save The Goose Project, the restoration of a very special Grumman Goose. The project began in 1988 with the development of a new museum in Ketchikan and the need for historical, local artifacts. Local aviation historian and artist, Don "Bucky" Dawson, had been fascinated with the Grumman Goose, the pilots who flew them, and the time period in which the Grumman Goose played such an important role in the lives of Ketchikan's people. The role the Goose played cannot be overstated; it had been the link between all of Southeast Alaska's communities as well as the outside world. Dawson began a four-year quest to locate a suitable Goose and the funds for its acquisition.

In February 1991, Canadian Trans Provincial Airlines had a recently ground-looped Goose for sale. Although damaged, the plane was certainly capable of being restored to pristine condition. After negotiation, the Goose was offered to the Tongass Historical Society for $75,000. Ironically, the Goose was none other than N88821, the very first Goose bought by Ellis Air Lines in 1946. The money to purchase the Goose was raised in just six weeks under the leadership of Bucky Dawson and included not one dollar of taxpayer money.

On November 8, 1992, the airframe was barged to Ketchikan in a great waterfront celebration capped off with a low flyby of three Grumman Goose aircraft in a "V" formation. Larry Teufel, a Portland businessman and Goose enthusiast, flew the lead plane. On his wings were Goose aircraft from the Royal Canadian Mounted Police and Trans Provincial Airlines. The Goose, N88821, is still undergoing restoration, which began with a complete teardown. Having acquired copies of Grumman's original engineering drawings enables project volunteers to fabricate the few parts not available from other sources. The Tongass Historical Society still needs funding for the project. In lieu of flowers at Dad's funeral, mourners were encouraged to make donations to the society for the continuing work on the Goose. The Goose will eventually be returned to static display, resplendent in original Ellis Airline-style colors.

The occasion was marked by videotaped interviews with legendary Goose pilots including Bob Ellis and Dad. Although Dad had many pleasant memories of the Goose, he did recall for the interviewer one experience that was not very enjoyable. It was a late afternoon flight from Juneau to Ketchikan with a full load of passengers. About fifty miles into the flight, Dad encountered a snowstorm, turned back, and almost immediately ran into more bad weather. He only had one choice: put it down somewhere and wait for better weather.

He did find a secluded bay, taxied up to the shore, and dropped anchor for what proved to be a very cold, unpleasant night — the most uncomfortable overnight he ever spent while flying a Goose.

Dad's last several years were happy ones, although he may have occasionally been lonely, but only briefly. He had his many friends and his weekly routines: driving out to the Goose project with his friend, Bert Linne, weekend visits to the Moose Club, and Sunday nights at the Derby Room. Visiting friends, such as the son of his old Ryan School buddy Bill Cass got the full guided tour: out to the Goose project, downtown, the Totem poles, Bodding breakfasts with toast made from homemade bread, the Yacht Club, dinner at the Moose Club, and afterwards lots of warm hospitality in his home.

About five years before Dad died, Eric's girlfriend Gina suggested that Thanksgiving for the Bodding family always be celebrated in Ketchikan with Dad. It was a wonderful idea and something we all, especially Dad, really appreciated.

Mom and Dad both enjoyed the special picnics in Edmonds, Washington. The picnics were essentially community events for people living in or originally from Juneau, Ketchikan, and Petersburg. During those visits, we tried to convince them to move down to the Seattle area, but they firmly chose to remain in Ketchikan. Even after Mom died, Dad continued to attend the community picnics and then visit with each of his children for several days. He last attended in 2005, thanks to Gina, whose enthusiasm and volunteering to escort him down from Ketchikan made the difference.

Travel eventually became a burden for Dad due to arthritis in one of his legs for which he had taken to using a cane. Like so many independent, senior citizens he was frustrated by automated check-in kiosks, Internet ticketing, waiting lines, airport security checks, and the impersonal nature of today's flying, especially compared to his airline days which were characterized by the ultimate in timely, personal service. In spite of the arthritis, he continued his annual trips to Las Vegas and southern California. With his pass, he could fly anywhere in the world for only the cost of tax on an airline ticket.

Only in his last year did Dad seem to slow down. Prior to 2005, he always had some major home improvement projects in progress. He spoke to us by phone each week. Still, he enjoyed many of the same routines that he and Mom shared: watching television, reading the newspaper, and making up fishing gear for Jim. While watching television, even when Mom was alive, Dad literally tied tens of thousands of short, twenty-inch pieces of twine into double-looped ganions, dying them, and putting a hook on each one. He continued tying them right up to the very end.

Dad always joked about living to, and then past, the age of eighty-five, his personally projected terminal launch date. "Don't kid yourself, it's the pits to get old," he would say. He never saw a doctor, declaring, "Why bother when all of my friends who have seen doctors are dead."

Dad was an active man right up to the day he died: May 6, 2006. On that last day, he got up early, made his bed, started making bread (which was found rising on the kitchen table), had coffee, his usual toast with peanut butter and jelly, and died suddenly next to his favorite chair. Dad's neighbor and good friend, Clyde Cowan, thought something was amiss when Dad's living room curtains remained open into the night. Normally, Dad always closed the curtains at sunset. Clyde found Dad and contacted the police who immediately notified us of Dad's passing. All three of us went up to Ketchikan the next day, and decided to hold off on the memorial service until late June, which would allow us to plan a better service as well as allow more family to attend.

Dad was not a formally religious person, but like a lot of pilots, he was spiritual. He thought that when a person dies, his spirit comes back in another way. When he saw a deer in the yard across the street, he would simply say that was one of his deceased buddies coming back to say "hello." After we all got back to the house after Dad died, we could not find a deer across the way, but there was a bald eagle sitting in the tree in the front yard. Eerily, the eagle was looking at our house and did not move for well over an hour. Quite obviously, it was Dad, still keeping an eye on us, making sure we that we were going to get things right.

He certainly lost none of his dry sense of humor in his old age. When we went through his house to put it in order, we found his financial and personal affairs right up to date, including his will, draft obituary, and funeral instructions (something simple, perhaps just a get together at the Moose Club). There was a file on each of us.

Appropriately, Jim's file included a recently tied black cod hook on a ganion. At the viewing, Jim slipped the ganion into the

The entire Bodding family enjoying Thanksgiving at Aunt Karen's hotel near Rinc'on de Guayabitos, Mexico, November 2007.

one of the pockets on the very-favored "Save the Goose" jacket Dad was wearing.

He also wanted to be cremated with his ashes being spread near the old Ellis Air Lines dock. Bucky Dawson, the prime mover and heart of the Save The Goose Project, said he would try to arrange for a Grumman Goose flyby at Dad's send-off, which we scheduled for late June when the weather promised to be better.

The morning of Dad's ceremony started rather gloomily, but soon the sun broke through. Bucky Dawson had assembled a small air fleet for Dad's last flight. Dad was to get his wishes because we dropped his ashes in the water just out from the old Ellis dock. Larry Teufel, the Portland businessman who had flown in the Save the Goose arrival ceremony in 1992 most graciously agreed to fly his Turbo Goose while Jim and Eric dispensed the ashes from the passenger compartment. Also in the Goose were Dad's two eldest grandchildren, Greg and Kimberly.

Moments after the ashes from the Goose fluttered down in the wind, a missing man formation consisting of six DeHavilland Beavers flew past, with the one Beaver peeling off in that ever so poignant maneuver right over the many people who had gathered on the dock.

Just a few moments before the ashes were released from the Goose, a large bald eagle flew right past the dock and returned moments after the thundering planes swept past, perching on the top of the Lutheran Church steeple where Mom and Dad had been married. Quite clearly, Dad's spirit was with us that day. Maybe thirty-four years before, when he made his last flight for Alaska to the west coast and was given his Tlingit and Haida names, he was given something else too.

The celebration continued, moving into the Moose Club while the pilots were landing. In addition to Larry in the Goose, the Beaver pilots were Steve Kamm, Jeff Carlin, Jim Vreeland, Ernie Robb, Jim Jakubek, and Michelle Masden. Once in the Moose Club, Jim led off by recalling some of his favorite memories of Dad, as did Eric and many friends. Capping off the day, which lasted much longer than anybody could have anticipated, was Bucky Dawson's memorial slide show, which captured Dad's early days, the war years, growing his family and the airline, and finally, becoming one of the grand old men of Ketchikan.

When we think of Dad, it is not of an elderly man walking with a cane; rather, it is of strong, good man in a pioneering, airline captain's uniform. He was essentially a modest man when it came to his accomplishments, but was very proud of the way he lived his life. He said that given a chance to do it all over again, he would change practically nothing. How few men can so close out their days.

JIM BODDING
ERIC BODDING
SHEILA BODDING HAYES

Index

Naval Reserve, 126
Navy Bureau of Personnel, 102
Scouting Squadron 70, 79
Transport Squadron 5, 114, 126
New Orleans, Louisiana, 110–111
North Sea, steamer, 22, 24, 68

O

O'Driscoll, Martha, 102
O'Riely, Mike (Secret Service), 106
Ordway, Fred, 18

P

Pacific Alaska Airways, 18, 71
Pacific Northern Airlines, 145
Palm Springs, California, 124
Pan American, 56, 71, 112, 126, 133, 145
Panhandle Air Transport, 22
Pasco, Washington, 112
Pennock Island, 136
Petersburg Air Service, 58, 59, 77, 131, 152
Petersburg, Alaska, 6, 22, 131, 133, 150, 154, 166
Port Angeles, Washington, 87
Portland, Oregon, 112
Pries, Bill, 57
Prince Rupert, British Columbia, 9, 71
Pusich, Rudy, 58

Q

Queen Charlotte Islands, 82–83
Queen Charlotte Sound, British Columbia, 61

R

Ramsdell, Hugh, 71, 130
Reeve Airways, 48
Reeve, Bob, 48, 53
Reeves, Admiral John, 82–83, 90, 98, 127
Renfro, Cmdr., 104
Rice, Lt. Cmdr, 82
Rinehart, Jim, 22
Robb, Ernie, 169
Robinson, Ray, 32
Roosevelt, President Franklin, 106–108
Roushman, Lt. Max, 121, 124
Royal Canadian Mounted Police, 165
Ryan School of Aeronautics, San Diego, California, 7, 37–46, 95

S

Salal Island, British Columbia, 64–70
Sande, Wes, 131, 135
San Diego, California, 58
Save the Goose! Project, 9–10, 164–165
Schwamm, Tony, 54, 58, 77, 131
Scott, ACRM Ray, 112
Scow Bay, 161, 164
Seattle, Washington, 22, 30–31, 59, 87, 95, 96, 131, 141, 145, 152, 154
SHEILA B (Bodding boat), 138–139
Sherman Harry, 50, 60–71
Sherman, Jack, 50, 60
Simmons, Shell, 9, 17, 22, 30–31, 35, 152
Sitka, 6, 31, 77, 150, 152, 154

Other HANCOCK HOUSE *aviation titles*

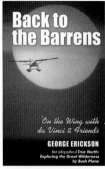

Back to the Barrens
George Erickson
978-0-88839-642-6
5½ x 8½, sc, 328 pages

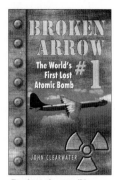

Broken Arrow #1
John Clearwater
978-0-88839-596-2
5½ x 8½, sc, 160 pages

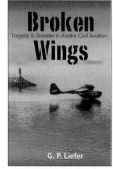

Broken Wings
G. P. Liefer
0-88839-524-8
5½ x 8½, sc, 304 pages

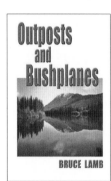

Outposts and Bushplanes
Bruce Lamb
0-88839-556-6
5½ x 8½, sc, 208 pages

Shaking the Feather Boa
E. C. (Ted) Burton
978-0-88839-609-9
5½ x 8½, sc, 192 pages

Wheels, Skis and Floats
E. C. (Ted) Burton &
Robert S. Grant
0-88839-428-4
5½ x 8½, sc, 176 pages

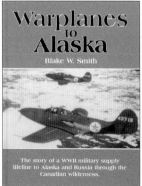

Warplanes to Alaska
Blake W. Smith
0-88839-401-2
8½ x 11, hc,
256 pages

**Wings Over
the Wilderness**
Blake W. Smith
978-0-88839-595-7
8½ x 11, sc,
296 pages

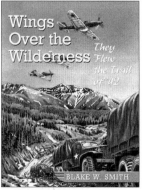